Book name

By Daniel Melehi

©December 2023

Contents

3

4

7

12

15

Introduction

Welcome to "**The Only Book You Will Ever Need for Making Money with No Code.**"

In this guide, we will explore the exciting world of no-code development and how it can help you create successful apps without any programming knowledge. In today's digital era, app development has become a lucrative market. However, traditionally, building an app required extensive coding skills or hiring expensive developers. That is where the no-code movement comes in. No-code platforms empower individuals with little to no coding experience to create their own apps and turn their ideas into reality. This book is designed to be a comprehensive resource for anyone interested in leveraging the potential of no-code development to build profitable apps. Whether you are a seasoned entrepreneur, a creative individual with a brilliant app idea, or a business owner looking to expand your digital presence, this book will equip you with the knowledge and tools you need to succeed. Throughout the chapters, we will explore various aspects of no-code development, starting from understanding the no-code movement to building your minimum viable product (MVP), designing user-centered apps, implementing monetization strategies, marketing and promotion, user acquisition and retention techniques, analytics and data-driven decision making, and much more. It is important to note that while no-code platforms have made app development more accessible, building a successful app still requires dedication, strategic thinking, and a strong understanding of your target audience. With the right approach and the guidance provided in this book, you can turn your app into a profitable venture. So, whether you are a novice or an experienced app developer, prepare yourself to dive into the world of no-code development, and get ready to transform your ideas into successful apps. Let's embark on this journey together and unlock the potential of no-code for financial success. Now, let's begin with Chapter 1: Understanding the No Code Movement.

Chapter 1: Understanding the No Code Movement

The technological landscape is evolving rapidly, and with it comes the emergence of the No Code movement. No Code refers to the ability to build applications and websites without writing traditional code, such as HTML, CSS, or JavaScript. This chapter will provide you with a comprehensive understanding of the No Code movement, its origins, and its significance in today's digital world.

THE RISE OF NO CODE

In recent years, the demand for software and digital solutions has skyrocketed. However, traditional software development processes often require extensive coding knowledge and expertise, making it challenging for individuals without a technical background to enter the market. This limitation has resulted in a significant gap between the demand for digital solutions and the supply of skilled developers. The No Code movement aims to bridge this gap by empowering individuals without coding skills to create their own applications. It provides a range of user-friendly tools and platforms that allow users to visually design and build functional applications through a graphical interface. No Code tools automate the coding process, enabling non-technical users to focus on designing their applications and bringing their ideas to life.

THE BENEFITS OF NO CODE

No Code offers several significant benefits, making it an attractive option for aspiring entrepreneurs, small businesses, and individuals looking to create their own digital projects. Some of these benefits include:

1. Increased Accessibility

No Code tools eliminate the technical barriers of traditional coding, enabling anyone with a computer and an internet connection to start building their applications. This accessibility empowers individuals from diverse backgrounds, regardless of their coding skills or resources, to turn their ideas into reality.

2. Time and Cost Efficiency

Traditional coding requires significant time and financial investments, as developers need to write code from scratch and often encounter complex debugging processes. No Code accelerates the development process by providing ready-made templates, drag-and-drop functionalities, and pre-built integrations. This reduces development time and costs, allowing entrepreneurs to bring their products to market faster and more affordably.

3. Flexibility and Iteration

No Code platforms facilitate rapid prototyping and iteration, enabling users to easily modify and improve their applications based on user feedback and market trends. This agility allows entrepreneurs to experiment with different ideas and pivot their products without the need for extensive coding changes.

4. Empowerment of Non-Technical Users

By removing the need for coding expertise, No Code tools empower non-technical users to take control of their projects. This democratization of software development enables individuals to solve real-world problems and transform their ideas into functional and user-friendly applications.

THE IMPACT OF NO CODE ON TRADITIONAL DEVELOPMENT

The No Code movement has sparked discussions and debates within the software development community. Critics argue that No Code might oversimplify the development process, leading to the creation of subpar applications. While it is true that No Code tools have limitations compared to custom-coded solutions, they offer a viable alternative for specific use cases, especially for startups, small businesses, and individuals with limited resources. No Code should not be seen as a replacement for traditional coding but rather as a complementary approach. No Code empowers non-technical individuals to build functioning applications quickly, while traditional coding is still necessary for complex systems and highly customized solutions.

CONCLUSION

The No Code movement is revolutionizing the way we approach software development and empowering individuals to turn their ideas into reality without the need for extensive coding knowledge. Understanding the principles and benefits of No Code will set the foundation for your journey in building successful applications using visual development tools. In the following chapters, we will explore different aspects of No Code, from choosing the right platform to monetization strategies, helping you navigate this exciting and rapidly evolving field. So let's dive in and unlock the possibilities that the No Code movement has to offer.

Chapter 2: Choosing the Right No Code Platform for Your App

Choosing the right no code platform for your app is a crucial step in the development process. With the rise of the no code movement, there are now numerous platforms available that empower individuals without coding skills to create their own applications. In this chapter, we will explore the factors to consider when selecting a no code platform for your app.

UNDERSTANDING YOUR APP'S REQUIREMENTS

Before diving into the selection process, it's important to have a clear understanding of your app's requirements. Consider the following questions:

What is the purpose of your app?

Identify the main goal or function of your app. Is it designed to solve a specific problem or provide a service? Defining the purpose will help you narrow down the type of no code platform you need.

What features and functionalities are necessary for your app?

Make a list of the essential features and functionalities you want your app to have. This could include user authentication, data storage, push notifications, payment integration, and more. Understanding your app's requirements will aid in evaluating the capabilities of different no code platforms.

What is your budget?

Consider your budget for the app development process. While no code platforms are generally more cost-effective compared to traditional coding, it's still important to have a clear budget in mind. Some no code platforms offer free plans with limited features, while others require a subscription or payment for advanced functionalities.

EVALUATING NO CODE PLATFORMS

Once you have a clear understanding of your app's requirements, it's time to start evaluating different no code platforms. Here are some key factors to consider:

Ease of use

One of the main advantages of no code platforms is their simplicity and user-friendly interfaces. Look for a platform that offers an intuitive drag-and-drop interface, allowing you to easily build and customize your app without the need for extensive coding or technical knowledge.

Customization options

Consider the level of customization options available on the platform. Can you easily modify the appearance and layout of your app? Can you integrate custom code if needed? The ability to personalize your app will ensure it aligns with your branding and design preferences.

Scalability

Think about the future growth and scalability of your app. Will the chosen no code platform be able to handle an increase in users and data volume? Look for platforms that offer scaling options, such as cloud hosting and automatic resource allocation, to ensure your app can handle increased demand.

Integrations

Evaluate the integration capabilities of the no code platform. Can it seamlessly integrate with third-party services and APIs? Consider the services you may need to integrate into your app, such as payment gateways, social media platforms, or analytics tools.

Support and community

Check the level of support provided by the no code platform. Do they offer documentation, tutorials, and a knowledge base? Is there an active community of users who can help answer questions and provide guidance? Good support and an engaged community can be invaluable resources when facing challenges during the app development process.

MAKING THE DECISION

Once you have evaluated different no code platforms based on the above factors, it's time to make a decision. Consider creating a pros and cons list for each platform, weighing the features, customization options, scalability, integrations, and support. Additionally, you may want to try out the platforms by building a small prototype or demo app to get a feel for their usability and capabilities. Remember, choosing the right no code platform is essential for the success of your app. Take the time to thoroughly evaluate your options and select a platform that aligns with your app's requirements, budget, and long-term goals. With the right platform in hand, you can unleash your creativity and bring your app idea to life without the need for traditional coding skills.

Chapter 3: Building Your Minimum Viable Product (MVP)

In this chapter, we will dive into the process of building a Minimum Viable Product (MVP) for your no code app. The MVP is a crucial step in the development process as it allows you to quickly validate your app idea and gather feedback from users. By starting with an MVP, you can minimize the risk and investment involved in building a fully-featured app.

UNDERSTANDING THE MINIMUM VIABLE PRODUCT (MVP)

Before we dive into the building process, let's first understand what an MVP is. The MVP is a version of your app that includes only the core features and functionalities required to solve a specific problem or address a particular need. It is not meant to be a complete, polished app, but rather a simplified version that can be developed rapidly and tested with real users. The main purpose of an MVP is to validate your assumptions and test the viability of your app idea in the real world. By launching an MVP, you can gather valuable feedback from early adopters, understand their pain points, and iterate based on their needs. This iterative process allows you to build a better and more refined app over time.

IDENTIFYING THE CORE FEATURES

When building an MVP, it's crucial to identify the core features that will drive the value of your app. These features should directly address the problem or need your app aims to solve. By focusing on the essentials, you can avoid getting overwhelmed and stay focused on delivering a functional and valuable product. To identify the core features, start by defining the main goal of your app. What is the primary problem you want to solve for your target audience? Once you have a clear goal in mind, brainstorm the features that will help achieve that goal. Keep in mind that each feature should provide value and contribute to the user experience.

CHOOSING THE RIGHT NO CODE COMPONENTS

Now that you have identified the core features, it's time to choose the right no code components to build your MVP. Most no code platforms offer a wide range of pre-built components, such as forms, databases, authentication modules, and integrations with third-party services. Evaluate the available components based on their suitability for your app's core features. Look for components that are customizable, easy to use, and align with your app's unique requirements. Consider the scalability and performance of the components, as well as the support provided by the platform.

DESIGNING THE USER INTERFACE

While building your MVP, you should also pay attention to the user interface (UI) design. A well-designed UI can greatly enhance the user experience and make your app more appealing to users. However, keep in mind that for an MVP, the focus should be on functionality rather than aesthetics. Use simple and intuitive UI elements to guide users through your app's core features. Avoid unnecessary clutter and complexity that could distract users from the main purpose of the app. With no code platforms, you can easily customize and iterate on your UI design as you gather feedback from users.

ITERATING AND IMPROVING

Once you have built your MVP, it's time to launch it and gather feedback from real users. Encourage users to provide feedback and collect data on their usage patterns, pain points, and suggestions for improvement. This feedback will be invaluable in guiding your future development efforts. Based on the feedback and data collected, prioritize the most valuable features and iterate on your app. Make incremental improvements and updates to address user needs and enhance the user experience. Remember, the MVP is just the starting point, and through iteration and continuous improvement, you can build a successful and robust app.

CONCLUSION

Building a Minimum Viable Product (MVP) is a critical step in the development process of your no code app. It allows you to quickly validate your app idea, gather feedback from users, and iterate based on their needs. By focusing on the core features, choosing the right components, and designing a user-friendly interface, you can build a functional MVP that sets the foundation for your app's success. Remember, the MVP is not the final version of your app, but rather a starting point for continuous improvement and refinement.

Chapter 4: User-Centered Design for No Code Apps

User-centered design is a critical aspect of creating successful no code apps. By prioritizing the needs and preferences of your target audience, you can develop an app that not only meets their expectations but also delivers an exceptional user experience. In this chapter, we will explore the key principles and best practices of user-centered design for no code apps.

THE IMPORTANCE OF USER RESEARCH

Before diving into the design process, it is crucial to gain a deep understanding of your target users. User research allows you to uncover their wants, needs, motivations, and pain points. By conducting interviews, surveys, and usability testing, you can collect valuable insights that will inform the design decisions you make.

Creating User Personas

User personas are fictional representations of your target users. They help you visualize and empathize with different user segments, allowing you to design with their specific needs in mind. When creating user personas for your no code app, consider factors such as demographics, behavior patterns, goals, and frustrations. These personas will serve as a foundation for your design decisions throughout the development process.

DESIGNING AN INTUITIVE USER INTERFACE

A user-friendly interface is crucial for the success of your no code app. Here are some key principles to keep in mind when designing the UI:

Simplicity:

Keep the interface clean and uncluttered. Avoid overwhelming users with too many options or complex navigation structures.

Stick to a minimalistic design that allows users to easily understand and access the app's features.

Consistency:

Maintain consistency throughout your app's design. Use standardized elements such as buttons, icons, and typography to create a familiar and intuitive experience for users. Consistency enhances usability and reduces cognitive load.

Visual Hierarchy:

Use visual hierarchy to guide users' attention and prioritize important elements on the screen. Establish a clear visual flow that leads users through the app and highlights key information.

Mobile-Friendly Design:

Given the increasing popularity of mobile devices, it is essential to design your no code app with mobile users in mind. Ensure that your app is responsive and provides a seamless experience across different screen sizes.

USABILITY TESTING

Usability testing is a crucial step in the user-centered design process. By observing how real users interact with your app, you can uncover usability issues, identify pain points, and gather insightful feedback. Consider conducting usability tests at different stages of development to iteratively improve your app's design and usability.

A/B Testing

A/B testing involves comparing two different versions of your app to see which one performs better. By testing different design elements, layouts, color schemes, and user flows, you can optimize your app's design based on empirical data. A/B testing allows you to make data-driven decisions and continuously refine your app's user experience.

ITERATIVE DESIGN AND CONTINUOUS IMPROVEMENT

User-centered design is an ongoing process. It involves continuously gathering feedback, analyzing user behavior, and making iterative improvements based on user insights. By incorporating user feedback and analytics data, you can refine your no code app over time, ensuring that it remains relevant and meets the evolving needs of your users.

Conclusion

User-centered design is essential for creating successful no code apps. By understanding your users, designing intuitive interfaces, conducting usability testing, and continuously iterating, you can build apps that deliver exceptional user experiences. Embrace user-centered design principles and make it a foundational aspect of your no code app development process.

Chapter 5: Testing and Debugging Your No Code App

Testing and debugging are crucial steps in the development process of any application, including those built with no code platforms. They ensure that your app functions as intended, meets the requirements, and provides a seamless user experience. In this chapter, we will explore the best practices for testing and debugging your no code app, along with the tools and techniques you can utilize.

IMPORTANCE OF TESTING

Testing allows you to identify and fix any issues or bugs in your no code app before it is released to users. It ensures that all functionalities work correctly, the user interface is responsive, and the app performs well across different devices and platforms. Testing also plays a vital role in determining the overall quality of your app, which directly impacts user satisfaction and engagement.

TYPES OF TESTING

There are several types of testing that you should consider when developing your no code app:

1. Functional Testing:

Functional testing verifies that each feature and functionality of your app works as intended. It involves testing user interaction, inputs, outputs, and the overall behavior of the app. Perform functional testing to ensure all buttons, links, forms, and other interactive elements function correctly without any errors or unexpected behavior.

2. Usability Testing:

Usability testing evaluates the ease of use and overall user experience of your app. It involves observing real users as they navigate through your app and complete tasks. Usability testing helps identify any usability issues, navigation problems, or areas where users may get confused. Collecting feedback from users during the usability testing phase can provide valuable insights for improving your app's design and functionality.

3. Performance Testing:

Performance testing measures how well your app performs under varying conditions, such as high traffic or limited network connectivity. It helps identify any performance bottlenecks, slow loading times, or resource-intensive components. By conducting performance testing, you can optimize your app's performance, ensuring it runs smoothly and efficiently for a better user experience.

4. Compatibility Testing:

Compatibility testing ensures that your no code app works seamlessly across different devices, operating systems, and web browsers. It is important to test your app on various platforms to ensure consistent functionality and appearance. Compatibility testing helps uncover any issues related to device-specific features, screen resolutions, or browser compatibility.

5. Security Testing:

Security testing is crucial to protect your app and users' data from potential vulnerabilities and threats. It involves testing for any weaknesses in your app's security measures, such as authentication, data encryption, or protection against common security risks. Conduct thorough security testing to ensure your app meets the necessary security standards and safeguards user information.

DEBUGGING TECHNIQUES

Debugging is the process of identifying, analyzing, and fixing issues or bugs in your app. Although no code platforms handle much of the underlying technical aspects, bugs can still occur due to incorrect configurations or incompatible components. Here are some effective debugging techniques for your no code app:

1. Divide and Conquer:

When faced with a bug, break down the problem into smaller parts and isolate the specific area where the issue occurs. By narrowing down the problem, you can focus your debugging efforts and identify the root cause more efficiently.

2. Use Logging and Error Handling:

Implement logging and error handling mechanisms in your app to capture detailed information about any errors or issues that may arise. This information can help you trace the source of the problem and understand the sequence of events leading to the error.

3. Utilize Developer Tools:

Most no code platforms provide developer tools or debugging consoles that allow you to inspect and troubleshoot your app's behavior. Take advantage of these tools to examine the code, monitor network requests, and debug any issues that may arise during runtime.

4. Test in Staging Environment:

Before releasing your app to production, test it in a staging environment that closely resembles the production environment. This allows you to identify and fix any issues that may occur in a controlled environment before they impact real users.

5. Gather User Feedback:

Encourage users to provide feedback on your app's performance and report any issues they encounter. User feedback can be invaluable in identifying bugs that may have been missed during testing. Promptly address user-reported issues and release bug fixes as part of regular updates to enhance your app's stability and user experience.

CONCLUSION

Testing and debugging are essential steps in ensuring the functionality, usability, performance, compatibility, and security of your no code app. By following the different testing techniques and utilizing effective debugging methods, you can identify and resolve any issues or bugs, leading to a smoother and more reliable user experience. Remember to continuously test and iterate on your app to maintain its quality and keep it running smoothly.

Chapter 6: Adding Functionality with Integrations

Adding functionality to your no code app is crucial for enhancing user experience and extending its capabilities. While no code platforms provide a wide range of built-in features, integrations can take your app to the next level by connecting it with external services, APIs, and databases. In this chapter, we will explore the power of integrations and how they can elevate your no code app.

UNDERSTANDING INTEGRATIONS

Integrations allow you to seamlessly combine the functionality of external services and tools with your no code app. They enable your app to interact with other platforms, exchange data, and perform additional tasks that are not available within the no code platform itself. Integrations come in various forms, such as API integrations, webhooks, database connections, and third-party tool integrations. These integrations can provide features like payment processing, email marketing automation, social media sharing, analytics tracking, and much more.

BENEFITS OF INTEGRATIONS

Integrating external services into your no code app offers several key benefits:

Expanded Functionality:

Integrations allow you to leverage the capabilities of established tools and services, enabling your app to perform advanced functions without any coding. This expands the possibilities for your app and enhances its overall functionality.

Time and Cost Savings:

By utilizing pre-built integrations, you can save time and money on development. Instead of building complex features from scratch, you can plug in existing solutions that have already been optimized and tested.

Increased Efficiency:

Integrating external services can automate various tasks and streamline workflows. For instance, integrating a customer relationship management (CRM) system can automate lead management and improve customer interactions, making your app more efficient and effective.

Access to Expertise:

Integrating with established services allows you to tap into the expertise of specialized providers. By utilizing their tools and services, you benefit from their experience and knowledge, even if you have limited coding skills or technical expertise.

CHOOSING THE RIGHT INTEGRATIONS

When selecting integrations for your no code app, it's essential to consider the specific needs and goals of your app. Here are some factors to keep in mind:

Compatibility:

Ensure that the integration is compatible with your chosen no code platform. Some platforms have predefined integrations, while others offer flexibility through custom integration options.

Functionality:

Assess the features and capabilities offered by the integration. Consider whether it aligns with your app's requirements and goals. Look for integrations that provide the specific functionality your app needs to enhance the user experience.

Reliability and Support:

Research the reputation of the integration provider. Look for reviews, testimonials, and customer support options to ensure that the integration is reliable and offers excellent support in case of any issues.

Scalability:

Consider the scalability of the integration. Will it be able to handle increased user traffic and data flow as your app grows? Choose integrations that can seamlessly grow with your app as it attracts more users.

Security:

Data security is crucial when integrating external services. Ensure that the integration provider has robust security measures in place to protect user data and comply with relevant regulatory standards.

IMPLEMENTING INTEGRATIONS IN YOUR NO CODE APP

Most no code platforms provide intuitive interfaces or integration marketplaces that make connecting external services a breeze. The process typically involves a few simple steps:

Authentication:

Provide the necessary credentials or API keys to establish a connection between your no code app and the integration provider.

Configuration:

Configure the integration settings according to your app's requirements. This may include mapping fields, setting up triggers or actions, and customizing specific functionalities.

Testing:

Test the integration thoroughly to ensure it functions as expected. Simulate various scenarios and evaluate the integration's performance and reliability.

Monitoring and Maintenance:

Regularly monitor the integration's performance and address any issues that arise. Stay updated with any updates or changes from the integration provider to ensure seamless functionality.

CONCLUSION

Integrations are valuable tools for adding functionality and extending the capabilities of your no code app. By integrating external services and tools, you can enhance user experience, streamline workflows, and unlock new possibilities. Remember to choose integrations that align with your app's requirements and goals, ensuring compatibility, reliability, scalability, and security. Implement integrations seamlessly using the intuitive interfaces provided by most no code platforms, and constantly monitor and maintain their performance for a seamless user experience.

Chapter 7: Monetization Strategies for No Code Apps

Generating revenue is a crucial aspect of any successful app, and monetization strategies for no code apps are no exception. While building an app with no code may save you time and money, it doesn't mean that you can't profit from your creation. In this chapter, we will explore various monetization strategies that you can implement to generate income from your no code app.

UNDERSTANDING MONETIZATION OPTIONS

Before diving into specific monetization strategies, it's essential to understand the different options available to you. Here are some common monetization models used in the app industry: 1. **Freemium:** This model offers a basic version of your app for free, while additional features and functionality are locked behind a paywall. Users have the option to upgrade to a premium version for a fee. 2. **In-App Purchases:** In-app purchases allow users to buy digital goods, extra content, or premium features within your app. This strategy is popular in gaming apps, but it can also be applied to other types of apps. 3. **Subscriptions:** Offering a subscription-based model allows users to access your app's features and content for a recurring fee. This model provides a steady stream of revenue and encourages long-term customer engagement. 4. **Advertising:** Integrating ads within your app can be a profitable monetization strategy. You can display various types of ads, such as banner ads, interstitial ads, or rewarded videos, and earn revenue based on user interactions or impressions. 5. **Affiliate Marketing:** This strategy involves promoting products or services within your app and earning a commission for each successful referral or sale. Affiliate marketing is particularly effective if your app is focused on a specific niche. 6. **Sponsorship:** In this model, you partner with brands or businesses to promote their products or services within your app. You can charge a sponsorship fee or receive commission-based incentives.

SELECTING THE RIGHT MONETIZATION STRATEGY

Choosing the most appropriate monetization strategy for your no code app depends on several factors, including your target audience, app's purpose, and your long-term goals. Here are some considerations to help you make an informed decision: 1. **App**

Category: Each app category has its own unique monetization opportunities. For example, gaming apps often rely on in-app purchases or advertising, while productivity apps may benefit from subscriptions or freemium models. 2. **User Preferences:** Understanding your target audience's preferences is crucial. Conduct market research and gather user feedback to identify which monetization models are more likely to resonate with your users. 3. **Value Proposition:** Assess the value your app provides to users. This will determine if users are more likely to pay for enhanced features or content, or if advertising and partnerships are a better fit. 4. **Competitor Analysis:** Study competitors in your niche to identify successful monetization strategies they have implemented. Additionally, learn from their mistakes and seek ways to differentiate yourself.

IMPLEMENTING MONETIZATION STRATEGIES IN NO CODE PLATFORMS

No code platforms typically provide built-in functionality and integrations that support various monetization strategies. Here are some ways you can implement monetization strategies in your no code app: 1. **Setting Up In-App Purchases:** Many no code platforms offer pre-built components for handling in-app purchases. These components allow you to easily create and manage products or content that users can purchase within your app. 2. **Integrating Ad Networks:** No code platforms often include integrations with popular ad networks, making it simple to display ads within your app. You can configure ad placements and track ad performance without the need for coding. 3. **Managing Subscriptions:** Some no code platforms offer features specifically designed for managing subscriptions. You can set up subscription plans, handle billing, and manage user access with ease. 4. **Utilizing Affiliate Marketing Tools:** While not all no code platforms offer built-in affiliate marketing functionality, you can integrate third-party tools to track referrals and manage affiliate campaigns. It's important to research and explore the capabilities of your chosen no code platform to ensure it can support your desired monetization strategies effectively.

Conclusion

Monetizing your no code app is a crucial step towards turning your project into a sustainable and profitable business. Understanding different monetization strategies, evaluating the suitability of each strategy, and selecting the appropriate one for your app's target audience and purpose are key aspects to consider. With the right approach and a well-executed monetization strategy, you can generate revenue and unlock the full potential of your no code app.

Chapter 8: Marketing and Promotion for Your No Code App

With your no code app built and ready to launch, it's time to shift your focus to marketing and promotion. While having a great app is crucial, without effective marketing, it may go unnoticed in the vast sea of applications. In this chapter, we will explore various strategies and techniques to market and promote your no code app. We will discuss the importance of defining your target audience, creating a strong brand identity, leveraging different marketing channels, utilizing social media, and measuring your marketing efforts.

DEFINING YOUR TARGET AUDIENCE

Defining your target audience is a crucial first step in your marketing journey. Understanding who your potential users are, their demographics, preferences, and pain points, will help you tailor your marketing messages and strategies. Begin by conducting market research and analyzing your competition. Identify the unique value proposition of your app and what sets it apart from others. This will enable you to position your app effectively and target the right audience. Creating User Personas can also help in visualizing and understanding your target audience. User Personas are fictional representations of your ideal users and help you tailor your marketing efforts to speak directly to their needs.

CREATING A STRONG BRAND IDENTITY

Building a strong brand identity is crucial for the success of your no code app. Your brand represents your values, your mission, and what your app stands for. It helps differentiate your app from competitors and creates a connection with users. Start by creating a memorable brand name and designing a unique logo that represents your app's essence. Use consistent branding elements such as colors, typography, and visual style across all marketing materials to create a cohesive brand presence. Craft a compelling brand story that communicates your app's purpose and resonates with your target audience. This story should highlight the problem your app solves and the benefits it offers.

LEVERAGING DIFFERENT MARKETING CHANNELS

To reach a wider audience and attract potential users, it's important to leverage various marketing channels. Here are some strategies to consider: 1. App Store Optimization (ASO): Optimize your app's presence in app stores by using relevant keywords, crafting compelling descriptions, and having high-quality app screenshots. 2. Content Marketing: Create valuable and informative content related to your app's niche. This can include blog posts, videos, podcasts, or infographics. Share this content through your website, social media platforms, and relevant online communities. 3. Influencer Marketing: Collaborate with influencers in your app's niche to reach their audience and gain credibility. This can involve sponsored content, partnerships, or reviews. 4. Email Marketing: Build an email list of interested users and regularly engage with them through newsletters, updates, and exclusive offers. 5. Paid Advertising: Invest in online advertising platforms such as Google Ads or social media ads to target specific demographics and promote your app.

UTILIZING SOCIAL MEDIA

Social media platforms are powerful tools for marketing your no code app. They allow you to engage with your audience, build a community, and create brand awareness. Here are some tips for utilizing social media effectively: 1. Choose the right platforms: Identify which social media platforms your target audience is active on and focus your efforts there. Common platforms include Facebook, Twitter, Instagram, LinkedIn, or TikTok. 2. Create engaging content: Share informative, entertaining, and visually appealing content related to your app. This can include behind-the-scenes peeks, tutorials, user testimonials, or industry news. 3. Interact with your audience: Respond to comments, messages, and reviews promptly. Encourage discussions, ask for feedback, and show appreciation for your users' support. 4. Run contests and giveaways: Promote user engagement by organizing contests, giveaways, or exclusive offers. This can help generate buzz and increase your app's visibility. 5. Collaborate with influencers: Partner with influencers relevant to your app's niche to reach their followers and gain credibility.

MEASURING YOUR MARKETING EFFORTS

Measuring the effectiveness of your marketing efforts is crucial to determine what strategies are working and make data-driven decisions. Here are some key metrics to track: 1. App Downloads: Monitor the number of app installs to gauge the success of your marketing efforts. 2. User Engagement: Track user engagement metrics such as session duration, screen views, and in-app actions. This will help you identify which features are popular and optimize your app accordingly. 3. Conversion Rates: Measure the conversion rates of your marketing campaigns. This can include the number of users who sign up, make in-app purchases, or subscribe to your services. 4. Social Media Metrics: Monitor metrics such as reach, engagement, likes, comments, and shares on your social media posts. This will help you understand which types of content resonate with your audience. 5. Customer feedback: Pay attention to user reviews, ratings, and feedback. This feedback can provide valuable insights into the user experience and help you improve your app. By tracking these metrics, you can assess the success of your marketing efforts, identify areas for improvement, and make informed decisions to drive growth.

Conclusion

Marketing and promoting your no code app is crucial for its success. By defining your target audience, creating a strong brand identity, utilizing various marketing channels, and measuring your efforts, you can effectively reach and engage potential users. Remember that marketing and promotion should be an ongoing process, and it's important to continuously refine your strategies based on user feedback and market trends.

Chapter 9: User Acquisition and Retention Techniques

User acquisition and retention are crucial for the success of any app, including those developed with no code platforms. In this chapter, we will explore various techniques and strategies to attract new users and keep them engaged with your app.

UNDERSTANDING USER ACQUISITION

User acquisition refers to the process of acquiring new users for your app. It involves targeted marketing efforts to attract individuals who are likely to become active users. Here are some effective user acquisition techniques:

1. App Store Optimization (ASO)

Optimizing your app's visibility in the app stores is essential for attracting new users. ASO involves optimizing your app's metadata, including the app title, description, keywords, and screenshots. By doing thorough research on relevant keywords and utilizing them strategically in your app's listing, you can improve its visibility in search results and increase the chances of attracting potential users.

2. Influencer Marketing

Collaborating with influencers can help you reach a wider audience and establish credibility for your app. Identify influencers in your app's niche and approach them for partnerships. Influencers can promote your app through sponsored content, reviews, or by simply sharing their positive experiences with your app. Their endorsement can significantly influence their followers and encourage them to download and try your app.

3. Content Marketing

Creating high-quality and informative content related to your app's niche can attract users organically. Consider starting a blog or creating engaging videos and tutorials that showcase the value of your app and address the pain points of your target audience. By optimizing this content for search engines and sharing it on relevant platforms, you can attract users who are actively seeking solutions within your app's domain.

4. Paid Advertising

Paid advertising can be an effective way to acquire new users quickly. Platforms such as Google Ads and social media platforms offer various advertising options, such as display ads, search ads, and sponsored posts. By carefully targeting your ads based on demographics, interests, and behaviors, you can reach potential users who are more likely to be interested in your app.

IMPLEMENTING USER RETENTION TECHNIQUES

User retention is just as important as user acquisition. Once you have acquired new users, it is crucial to keep them engaged and satisfied to prevent churn. Here are some user retention techniques to consider:

1. Personalization

Personalizing the user experience can significantly enhance user engagement and satisfaction. Tailor your app's content, recommendations, and notifications based on user preferences and behaviors. Leverage user data to provide a personalized experience that addresses individual needs, ultimately building a long-term relationship with your users.

2. Gamification

Introducing game-like elements and mechanics into your app can make it more enjoyable and addictive for users. Implement features such as achievements, leaderboards, badges, and rewards to incentivize users to engage with your app regularly. By creating a sense of competition or accomplishment, you can improve user retention and encourage users to reach specific milestones within your app.

3. Push Notifications

Utilize push notifications to keep users informed about updates, new features, promotions, or personalized recommendations. However, be mindful of not overwhelming users with excessive notifications. Ensure that your notifications are relevant, valuable, and tailored to individual user preferences. Effective use of push notifications can drive users back to your app and remind them of its value.

4. Regular Updates and Bug Fixes

Continuously improving your app by releasing regular updates and bug fixes demonstrates your commitment to providing an excellent user experience. Address user feedback and address any technical issues promptly to ensure a seamless and error-free experience. By keeping your app updated and bug-free, you build trust and loyalty with your users.

5. Customer Support and Communication

Offering exceptional customer support and maintaining open lines of communication with your users can significantly impact user retention. Provide multiple channels for users to reach out to you, such as email, live chat, or social media. Respond promptly to inquiries, address concerns, and listen to user feedback. By showing that you value their input and care about their experience, you can build long-term relationships with your users.

CONCLUSION

User acquisition and retention are essential for the success of your no code app. By implementing effective user acquisition techniques and utilizing various strategies to keep users engaged and satisfied, you can grow your user base, increase app downloads, and build a loyal user community. Remember to continuously refine your user acquisition and retention strategies based on user feedback, market trends, and the specific needs of your app's target audience.

Chapter 10: Analytics and Data-Driven Decision Making

In today's digital world, data is abundant and readily available. By harnessing the power of analytics and data-driven decision making, you can gain valuable insights into how your no code app is performing, understand user behavior, and make informed decisions to drive success.

THE IMPORTANCE OF ANALYTICS

Analytics provide a deeper understanding of your app's performance, user engagement, and conversion rates. By analyzing data, you can identify patterns, trends, and areas for improvement. Without analytics, you would be operating in the dark, lacking the insights needed to make informed decisions.

Key Metrics to Track

When it comes to analytics, there are several key metrics that you should track to gain valuable insights into your app's performance: 1. User Acquisition: Understanding how users are discovering and downloading your app is crucial. Track metrics such as app store impressions, downloads, and conversion rates to measure the effectiveness of your user acquisition strategies. 2. User Engagement: Evaluate metrics such as session duration, screen views, and in-app actions to gauge user engagement with your app. This data can help you identify areas where users are interacting most and where improvements can be made. 3. Retention Rate: Retaining users is essential for the long-term success of your app. Monitor metrics such as daily, weekly, and monthly retention rates to identify any patterns or drop-offs in user engagement. This data can guide you in implementing strategies to improve user retention. 4. Conversion Rate: If your app offers in-app purchases, subscriptions, or other monetization strategies, tracking the conversion rate is crucial. This metric measures the percentage of users who convert from free to paid services. By analyzing this data, you can optimize your monetization strategies and increase revenue. 5. Funnel Analysis: Funnels allow you to visualize the user journey from initial engagement to desired actions. By tracking each step in the funnel, you can identify points of friction or drop-off and make improvements to optimize the user experience.

DATA-DRIVEN DECISION MAKING

Making decisions based on data rather than relying solely on intuition can lead to more informed and successful outcomes. Here are some key principles to follow when using analytics for data-driven decision making:

Set Clear Goals

Before diving into data analysis, establish clear goals for your app. Define key performance indicators (KPIs) that align with your overall business objectives. These goals will serve as benchmarks for measuring success and guide the data analysis process.

Collect and Analyze Data

Implement analytics tools such as Google Analytics, Mixpanel, or Firebase to collect relevant data points. These tools provide insightful reports and visualizations that can help you gain deep insights into user behavior. Analyze the data regularly and identify trends, patterns, and areas for improvement.

Iterate and Experiment

Use data to drive your decision making and continuously iterate and experiment with different strategies. Test variations of app features, designs, or marketing campaigns to determine what works best for your target audience. By measuring the impact of these experiments through data analysis, you can optimize your app's performance and drive better results.

Monitor and Adjust

Regularly monitor the key metrics and performance indicators you established earlier. Pay attention to any significant changes or deviations from your goals. If you notice any trends or issues, take prompt action to adjust your strategies accordingly.

Make Informed Decisions

When it comes to making decisions for your no code app, use data as your guide. Consider the insights gained from analytics along with other factors such as user feedback, market trends, and industry best practices. By combining these inputs, you can make informed decisions that are more likely to lead to success.

CONCLUSION

Analytics and data-driven decision making are crucial for optimizing the performance of your no code app. By continually monitoring key metrics, analyzing data, and making informed decisions based on insights, you can drive success, improve user engagement, and increase revenue.

Embrace the power of analytics and leverage data to continuously refine and enhance your app.

Chapter 11: Optimizing Performance and Scalability

In today's fast-paced digital world, users have high expectations when it comes to app performance and scalability. To ensure the success of your no code app, it is crucial to optimize its performance and make it capable of handling increased demand. This chapter will guide you through the steps of optimizing performance and scalability for your no code app.

UNDERSTANDING PERFORMANCE OPTIMIZATION

Performance optimization involves improving the speed, responsiveness, and overall efficiency of your app. It ensures that users have a smooth and seamless experience while using your app. Here are some key strategies for optimizing performance:

Clean and Efficient Code

Even though you are building your app using a no code platform, it is still important to write clean and efficient code. This means avoiding unnecessary and redundant code and making sure that your app follows best practices for performance.

Caching

Caching is the process of storing commonly accessed data in temporary storage, such as in-memory cache or browser cache. By caching static content, you can reduce the load on your app's servers and significantly improve its performance.

Image Optimization

Images are often the heaviest assets in an app and can slow down its performance. To optimize image loading times, consider compressing images without compromising their quality, using lazy loading techniques, and utilizing responsive images that are appropriate for different screen sizes.

Minification and Compression

Minification involves removing unnecessary characters and whitespace from your app's code, making it more compact and efficient. Compression, on the other hand, reduces the size of your app's files by compressing them. Both minification and compression help to improve your app's performance by reducing the amount of data that needs to be downloaded.

ENSURING SCALABILITY

Scalability refers to the ability of your app to handle increased traffic and user demand without sacrificing performance. Here are some strategies for ensuring scalability:

Load Balancing

Load balancing involves distributing incoming network traffic across multiple servers to ensure that no single server gets overloaded. By implementing load balancing techniques, you can distribute the workload evenly and improve your app's ability to handle increased traffic.

Elastic Infrastructure

Utilizing cloud-based infrastructure, such as Amazon Web Services (AWS) or Google Cloud Platform, allows you to easily scale your app's resources up or down based on demand. With an elastic infrastructure, you can dynamically adjust server capacity to handle traffic spikes and ensure a seamless user experience.

Database Optimization

Optimizing your app's database can significantly improve its scalability. Ensure that your database is properly indexed, use caching techniques to reduce database queries, and consider implementing sharding or partitioning to distribute the data across multiple servers.

Monitoring and Performance Testing

Regularly monitoring your app's performance and conducting performance testing is essential for identifying potential bottlenecks and improving scalability. Use tools like New Relic, Datadog, or Google Analytics to track your app's performance metrics and identify areas for improvement.

CONCLUSION

Optimizing performance and scalability is crucial for the success of your no code app.

By following the strategies and techniques outlined in this chapter, you can ensure that your app provides a seamless user experience, even during periods of increased demand. Continuously monitoring and refining your app's performance and scalability will contribute to its success in the long run.Designing for Different Devices and Screen Sizes When developing a no code app, it's important to consider the diversity of devices and screen sizes that your users may have. Designing with mobile-first in mind has become increasingly important as mobile usage continues to rise. In this chapter, we will explore the principles and best practices for designing your no code app to be responsive and adaptive to different devices and screen sizes. 1. Understanding Responsive Design: Responsive design is an approach to web design that aims to provide an optimal viewing and interaction experience across different devices and screen sizes. It allows your app to adapt and respond to the user's device, whether it's a smartphone, tablet, or desktop computer. With responsive design, your app's layout, images, and content will automatically adjust and reflow to fit the screen size, ensuring a seamless and user-friendly experience. 2. Mobile-First Design: Mobile-first design is a responsive design approach that prioritizes the mobile user experience. It involves designing and developing your app with the smallest screen size in mind and then progressively enhancing it for larger screens. By starting with mobile design, you ensure that your app is optimized for the majority of users who access it on mobile devices. 3. Designing Flexible Layouts: When designing for different screen sizes, it's important to create flexible layouts that can adapt to various resolutions. This can be achieved by using relative units of measurement, such as percentages and ems, instead of fixed pixels. Additionally, employing CSS media queries allows you to specify different styles and layout rules based on the device's screen size. 4. Content Prioritization: With limited screen real estate on mobile devices, it's crucial to prioritize content and display only the essential information. Consider the needs and context of your users when deciding what content to include and how to present it. Utilize techniques such as collapsible menus, accordions, and tabbed navigation to organize and hide content that is not immediately relevant or important. 5. Touch-Friendly Interactions: As mobile devices rely heavily on touch interactions, ensuring that your app's elements are touch-friendly is essential. Use larger buttons and interactive elements that are easily tappable with a finger. Provide adequate spacing between elements to prevent accidental taps. Avoid small font sizes and fine details that may be difficult to interact with on smaller screens. 6. Consistency Across Devices: While designing for different devices and screen sizes, it's important to maintain consistency in branding, user interface elements, and navigation throughout your app. Consistency builds familiarity and helps users navigate your app seamlessly across different devices. Use the same color palette, typography, and design patterns across all screen sizes to create a cohesive and unified experience. 7. Multi-Device Testing: To ensure that your app looks and functions as intended on various devices, it's essential to conduct thorough testing on different screen sizes. Use device simulators, emulators, and real devices to test your app's responsiveness and adaptability. Pay close attention to layout distortions, text readability, button sizes, and touch interactions during the testing process. 8. Iterative Design and Optimization: Designing for different devices and screen sizes is an iterative process. Continuously gather user feedback and data to identify areas for improvement and optimization. Analyze user behavior patterns, user flow, and conversion rates to make data-driven design decisions. Regularly update and refine your app's design based on user feedback and evolving device trends. By following these principles and best practices, you can ensure that your no code app provides a seamless and visually appealing user experience across different devices and screen sizes. Designing for responsiveness and adaptability not only enhances user satisfaction but also increases the accessibility and reach of your app.

Chapter 13: Implementing In-App Purchases and Subscription Models

In the world of app monetization, in-app purchases and subscription models have become highly popular and effective strategies for generating revenue. By offering additional features, content, or virtual goods within your app, you can provide value to your users while creating a sustainable business model. In this chapter, we will explore the various aspects of implementing in-app purchases and subscription models in your no code app.

UNDERSTANDING IN-APP PURCHASES

In-app purchases refer to the ability for users to buy additional content or features within your app. This can include items such as virtual goods, premium content, or ad-free experiences. In order to implement in-app purchases in your no code app, you will need to integrate a payment gateway that supports these transactions. When implementing in-app purchases, it is important to carefully consider the user experience. Make sure that the purchase process is seamless and intuitive, and clearly communicate the benefits of the purchase to the user. Additionally, be transparent about the pricing and ensure that users have a hassle-free way to manage their purchases, such as the ability to restore purchases or manage subscriptions.

INTEGRATING SUBSCRIPTION MODELS

Subscription models offer users access to premium content or features for a recurring fee. This can provide a stable and predictable revenue stream for your app. Implementing subscription models in your no code app will also require integration with a payment gateway that supports recurring billing. When designing your subscription offerings, it is important to strike a balance between providing value to your users and setting a fair price. Consider offering different subscription tiers with varying levels of access or benefits. Additionally, make sure to clearly communicate the terms of the subscription, such as the duration, renewal process, and any cancellation policies.

IMPLEMENTING THE TECHNICAL ASPECTS

Implementing in-app purchases and subscription models in your no code app will require leveraging the tools and capabilities provided by your chosen no code platform. Many no code platforms offer built-in functionality and integrations for implementing these monetization strategies. To get started, you will need to connect your app to a payment gateway that supports in-app purchases and subscription billing. This typically involves setting up an account with the payment gateway provider and configuring the necessary API keys or credentials within your no code platform. Once you have integrated the payment gateway, you will need to define the products or subscriptions that you want to offer in your app. This involves specifying the pricing, payment intervals, and any associated features or benefits for each offering. Depending on your no code platform, you may be able to visually configure these products or subscriptions using a drag-and-drop interface. Finally, you will need to handle the purchase or subscription confirmation process within your app. This typically involves providing a seamless and secure payment flow for users, handling any necessary verifications or validations, and notifying your app of successful purchases or renewals.

BEST PRACTICES FOR IMPLEMENTING IN-APP PURCHASES AND SUBSCRIPTION MODELS

To ensure the success of your in-app purchases and subscription models, consider the following best practices:

1. Provide Value

Make sure that your in-app purchases or subscription offerings provide clear value to your users. Offer additional features, content, or benefits that enhance the user experience and solve their pain points.

2. Test and Iterate

Regularly test and iterate on your in-app purchases and subscription models based on user feedback and data. Monitor user adoption and engagement with these monetization features and make adjustments as necessary.

3. Offer Trial Periods

Consider offering trial periods for your subscription models to allow users to experience the value before committing to a payment. This can encourage adoption and reduce friction in the decision-making process.

4. Implement Cancellation Policies

Clearly communicate your app's cancellation policies and make it easy for users to cancel their subscriptions if needed. Providing a hassle-free cancellation process can help build trust and loyalty with your users.

5. Provide Customer Support

Offer excellent customer support for users who have questions or issues with their in-app purchases or subscriptions. Make it easy for them to reach out through various channels, such as email or live chat.

6. Stay Compliant with App Store Guidelines

Ensure that your implementation of in-app purchases and subscription models follows the guidelines set by app stores such as Apple's App Store or Google Play Store. Failure to comply with these guidelines could result in your app being removed from the store.

CONCLUSION

Implementing in-app purchases and subscription models can be a powerful way to monetize your no code app. By providing additional value to your users and creating a sustainable business model, you can generate revenue and drive the growth of your app. When implementing these features, consider the user experience, carefully design your offerings, and continuously iterate based on user feedback and market trends.

Chapter 14: Leveraging Social Media for App Success

Social media has become an integral part of our lives, offering countless opportunities to connect, share, and promote. Leveraging the power of social media is essential for app success in today's digital landscape. By utilizing social media platforms strategically, you can reach a wider audience, increase brand visibility, engage with users, and drive downloads and user acquisition. In this chapter, we will explore various strategies and best practices for leveraging social media effectively to promote and grow your no code app.

1. CHOOSE THE RIGHT SOCIAL MEDIA PLATFORMS

There are numerous social media platforms available today, each with its own unique audience and features. It is crucial to identify and choose the platforms that align with your target audience and app niche. Consider factors such as user demographics, engagement levels, and the platform's suitability for visual or text-based content. For example, if your app targets a younger audience, platforms like Instagram and TikTok may be more effective. On the other hand, if your app caters to professionals or B2B users, platforms like LinkedIn might be more suitable. Research and analyze user data to inform your decision and focus your efforts on platforms where your target audience is most active.

2. BUILD A STRONG BRAND PRESENCE

A strong and consistent brand presence on social media is essential for app success. Establishing a recognizable brand identity helps build trust and fosters engagement with your target audience. It is important to create a cohesive brand experience across all social media platforms. Create visually appealing profiles that reflect your app's aesthetic and values. Use consistent branding elements such as your logo, color palette, and typography. Craft an engaging bio that clearly communicates your app's value proposition and unique selling points. Share compelling and relevant content that resonates with your audience. Use a mix of promotional content, informative posts, behind-the-scenes glimpses, user-generated content, and interactive elements.

Encourage user engagement by asking questions, posting polls, and running contests or giveaways.

3. ENGAGE AND INTERACT WITH YOUR AUDIENCE

Social media is a two-way communication channel, and it is important to engage and interact with your audience. Respond promptly to comments, direct messages, and mentions. Show genuine interest in your users' feedback, questions, and concerns. Encourage conversations and create a sense of community around your app. Leverage social media features such as live streaming, Instagram Stories, or Twitter threads to provide real-time updates, share tips, or conduct Q&A sessions. Use hashtags relevant to your app niche to increase discoverability and join relevant conversations. Collaborate with influencers or power users in your industry to expand your reach and credibility.

4. LEVERAGE USER-GENERATED CONTENT

User-generated content (UGC) is a powerful tool for social media marketing. Encourage your app users and followers to create and share content related to your app. This could include reviews, testimonials, tutorials, or creative posts featuring your app. UGC provides social proof and builds trust among potential users. Regularly monitor social media platforms for mentions of your app and user-generated content. Engage with and repost high-quality content, giving credit to the creator. Highlight user stories or experiences that showcase the value and benefits of your app. This not only helps in promoting your app but also strengthens the bond with your existing users.

5. ANALYZE AND OPTIMIZE YOUR SOCIAL MEDIA EFFORTS

To ensure the effectiveness of your social media strategies, it is important to analyze and optimize your efforts. Regularly review social media analytics and insights to track key metrics such as engagement, reach, follower growth, and website traffic. Identify patterns, trends, and opportunities for improvement. A/B test different types of content, posting schedules, or call-to-action strategies to refine your approach. Use social media management tools to schedule posts in advance, monitor conversations, and measure performance. Stay updated with the latest social media best practices and algorithm changes to adapt your strategy accordingly.

Conclusion

Leveraging social media effectively can greatly contribute to the success and growth of your no code app. By choosing the right platforms, building a strong brand presence, engaging with your audience, leveraging user-generated content, and continuously analyzing and optimizing your efforts, you can maximize the impact of social media on your app's visibility, user acquisition, and overall success. Social media provides a powerful avenue for promoting your app, connecting with your audience, and staying ahead in the competitive app market.

Chapter 15: Utilizing Push Notifications to Engage Users

Push notifications are a powerful tool for engaging and retaining users in your no code app. With push notifications, you can send timely and relevant messages directly to your users' devices, even when they are not actively using your app. This allows you to keep your users informed, engaged, and coming back for more. In this chapter, we will explore the benefits of push notifications and how to effectively implement them in your no code app.

THE BENEFITS OF PUSH NOTIFICATIONS

Push notifications offer several benefits for engaging users in your no code app: 1. **Improved User Engagement:** Push notifications can help increase user engagement by sending targeted and personalized messages to your users. By delivering relevant content, updates, and promotions, you can encourage users to open your app and take specific actions. 2. **Increased Retention:** Push notifications can help improve user retention by reminding users to revisit your app and providing value even when they are not actively using it. Regularly sending updates and relevant information can keep users engaged and prevent them from uninstalling your app. 3. **Real-Time Communication:** Push notifications enable real-time communication with your users. Whether you want to inform users about new features, promotions, or important updates, push notifications allow you to instantly reach your users' devices, ensuring that your message is seen in a timely manner. 4. **Personalization:** Push notifications can be personalized based on user preferences, behavior, and location. By leveraging user data, you can tailor your messages to specific segments of your user base, increasing the relevancy and effectiveness of your notifications.

IMPLEMENTING PUSH NOTIFICATIONS IN YOUR NO CODE APP

Implementing push notifications in your no code app can be achieved through integrations with third-party services that offer push notification functionality. Here's a step-by-step guide on how to implement push notifications in your no code app: 1. **Choose a Push Notification Service:** Research and choose a push notification service that integrates with your chosen no code platform. Popular options include OneSignal, Firebase Cloud Messaging, and Pusher. 2. **Set up API Keys or Credentials:** Follow the documentation provided by the push notification service to set up API keys or credentials required for integration with your app. These keys will be used to authenticate and authorize your app to send push notifications. 3. **Integrate the Push Notification Service:** Depending on your no code platform, there may be built-in integration options for popular push notification services. Follow the platform's documentation on how to integrate the push notification service with your app. This may involve adding API keys, configuring settings, and setting up event triggers. 4. **Define Notification Triggers:** Determine the events or actions in your app that will trigger a push notification. For example, you may want to send a push notification when a user receives a new message, when there is an important update or announcement, or when a user's subscription is about to expire. **5. Create Notification Templates:** Design and create notification templates that will be used for different types of notifications. Consider using personalized content, appealing images, and clear calls to action to make your notifications engaging and actionable. **6. Segment and Target Your Audience:** Leverage user data and segmentation capabilities provided by the push notification service to target specific groups of users with relevant and personalized messages. You can segment users based on their preferences, behavior, location, or any other relevant criteria. **7. Test and Iterate:** Before sending push notifications to your entire user base, test your notifications on a small group of users to ensure they are working as intended. Gather feedback and iterate on your notifications based on user responses and engagement metrics. **8. Monitor and Analyze:** Once your push notifications are live, monitor the performance and engagement metrics of your notifications. Track metrics such as open rates, click-through rates, and conversions to measure the effectiveness of your notifications. Use this data to fine-tune your notifications and optimize their impact.

BEST PRACTICES FOR EFFECTIVE PUSH NOTIFICATIONS

To ensure that your push notifications are effective and well-received by your users, consider the following best practices: 1. **Keep Notifications Relevant:** Only send push notifications that are timely and relevant to your users. Avoid spamming users with irrelevant messages, as this can lead to users disabling notifications or uninstalling your app. 2. **Personalize and Segment:** Leverage user data to personalize your push notifications and segment your audience. Delivering personalized content based on user preferences and behavior can significantly improve engagement and conversion rates. 3. **Design Engaging**

Notifications: Use eye-catching visuals, clear and concise messaging, and compelling calls to action in your push notifications. Ensure that your notifications are visually appealing and aligned with your app's branding. 4. **Optimize Timing:** Consider the timing of your push notifications to maximize engagement. Avoid sending notifications during late-night hours or times when users are unlikely to engage with your app. Experiment with different times and days to determine the optimal timing for your target audience. 5. **A/B Test:** Test different variations of your push notifications to identify the most effective strategies. Experiment with different messaging, visuals, and call-to-action buttons to optimize your notifications for engagement and conversion. 6. **Monitor Performance Metrics:** Continuously monitor and analyze the performance metrics of your push notifications. Track open rates, click-through rates, and conversions to understand the effectiveness of your notifications. Use this data to iterate and improve your future notification campaigns. 7. **Respect User Preferences:** Allow users to customize their notification preferences within your app. Provide options for users to choose the types of notifications they want to receive and the frequency of notifications. Respect user preferences and avoid overloading users with excessive notifications. Incorporating push notifications into your no code app can significantly enhance user engagement and retention. By leveraging these powerful tools effectively, you can keep your users informed, engaged, and coming back for more. Remember to follow best practices and monitor the performance of your push notifications to continuously improve and refine your strategies.

Chapter 16: Implementing User Feedback and Iterating

User feedback is a valuable resource for improving your no code app and ensuring it meets the needs and expectations of your users. Implementing and effectively utilizing user feedback can lead to a more successful and user-centric app experience. In this chapter, we will explore the importance of user feedback, how to gather it, and how to iterate and make updates based on the feedback received.

THE IMPORTANCE OF USER FEEDBACK

User feedback provides valuable insights into what is working well in your app and what can be improved. By listening to your users, you can gain a better understanding of their needs, pain points, and preferences. Here are some key reasons why user feedback is important: 1. Identifying usability issues: Users can help uncover any usability issues or difficulties they encounter while using your app. Their feedback can highlight areas where the app may be confusing or frustrating to navigate. 2. Discovering new features or improvements: Users often have great ideas for new features or improvements that you may not have considered. Their feedback can spark innovation and guide your development process. 3. Building customer loyalty: By actively seeking and responding to user feedback, you show your users that their opinions matter. This increases their trust and loyalty to your app, leading to higher user retention. 4. Gaining a competitive edge: User feedback can provide valuable insights into your competitors' strengths and weaknesses. By understanding the gaps in the market, you can make strategic improvements to differentiate your app.

GATHERING USER FEEDBACK

To effectively implement user feedback, you need to have a reliable process in place for collecting and analyzing feedback. Here are some methods you can use to gather user feedback: 1. In-app feedback forms: Implement feedback forms within your app, allowing users to submit their thoughts and suggestions directly. Keep the form simple and concise to encourage more responses. 2. Surveys and questionnaires: Conduct targeted surveys to gather specific feedback on certain features or aspects of your app. Use tools like Google Forms or SurveyMonkey to create and distribute surveys. 3. User interviews and focus groups: Engage with a group of users in a more in-depth manner through interviews or focus groups. This allows you to have a more personal and detailed conversation to gather qualitative feedback. 4. App store reviews and ratings: Monitor and analyze the reviews and ratings users leave on your app's listing page in app stores. These can provide valuable insights into what users like and dislike about your app. 5. Social media listening: Monitor social media platforms, online forums, and communities related to your app's niche. Pay attention to any discussions or comments about your app to gain insights and respond to user concerns.

ITERATING AND MAKING UPDATES

Once you have collected user feedback, it's important to take action and make iterative updates to improve your app. Here are key steps to consider when implementing user feedback: 1. Analyze feedback trends: Look for common themes or patterns in the feedback you receive. Identify the most critical issues or requested features that will have the biggest impact on user satisfaction. 2. Prioritize updates: Based on the analysis, prioritize the updates you need to make. Consider the impact, feasibility, and resources required for each update. 3. Develop a roadmap: Create a roadmap for implementing the updates, outlining the specific features or improvements you plan to work on. This helps keep your team focused and provides a timeline for release. 4. Communicate with users: Keep your users informed about the updates and improvements you are making based on their feedback. Regularly communicate with them through app updates, release notes, and in-app messages. 5. Test and iterate: Before releasing updates, conduct thorough testing to ensure the changes address the user feedback effectively. Iterate based on user testing and gather feedback throughout the testing phase. 6. Monitor and evaluate: Once updates are released, closely monitor how users respond to the changes. Use analytics tools to track metrics like user engagement, retention, and satisfaction. Analyze the impact of the updates and make further adjustments if necessary.

CONCLUSION

Implementing user feedback and iterating based on user insights is crucial for creating a user-centric app that meets the needs and expectations of your target audience. By actively listening to your users and making continuous improvements, you can build a loyal user base, maintain a competitive edge, and drive the success of your no code app. In the next chapter, we will explore how to adapt to changing technology and trends in the fast-paced world of no code development.

Chapter 17: Adapting to Changing Technology and Trends

Technology is constantly evolving, and trends come and go. As a no code developer, it is crucial to adapt to these changes to stay relevant and ensure the success of your app. In this chapter, we will explore strategies for adapting to changing technology and trends in the world of no code development.

1. STAY UP-TO-DATE WITH THE LATEST TECHNOLOGY

To adapt to changing technology, it is essential to stay informed about the latest advancements and updates in the field of no code development. Follow industry blogs, attend webinars and conferences, join online communities, and engage in discussions with fellow developers. By staying up-to-date, you can identify emerging technologies and incorporate them into your app.

2. EMBRACE NEW FEATURES AND FUNCTIONALITY

No code platforms are constantly improving and adding new features and functionality. As updates are released, take the time to explore and understand the new capabilities they offer. Consider how these features can enhance your app and improve the user experience. By embracing new features and functionality, you can stay ahead of the competition and provide innovative solutions to your users.

3. MONITOR MARKET TRENDS

In addition to keeping up with technology, it is important to monitor market trends. Stay informed about what users are looking for in an app and what competitors are offering. Analyze user feedback, conduct market research, and keep an eye on industry reports. By understanding market trends, you can make informed decisions about the direction of your app and implement features that align with user preferences.

4. EXPERIMENT AND ITERATE

Adapting to changing technology and trends often involves experimentation and iteration. Don't be afraid to try new ideas and approaches. Test different features, designs, and functionalities to see how they resonate with your users. Gather feedback and iterate based on user insights. By continuously experimenting and iterating, you can refine your app and ensure it remains fresh and relevant.

5. COLLABORATE WITH OTHER DEVELOPERS

Collaboration is key to adapting to changing technology. Engage with other no code developers, share knowledge, and learn from each other's experiences. Collaboration can lead to new ideas, insights, and perspectives. Join online communities, attend meetups, and participate in hackathons to connect with like-minded individuals. By collaborating with others, you can stay at the forefront of no code development trends.

6. FUTURE-PROOF YOUR APP

While it is impossible to predict the future of technology, you can take steps to future-proof your app. This includes designing your app with scalability in mind, considering compatibility with emerging technologies, and building a flexible architecture. By future-proofing your app, you can adapt to new technologies and trends as they arise without major disruptions.

CONCLUSION

Adapting to changing technology and trends is crucial for the success of your no code app. Stay up-to-date with the latest technology, embrace new features and functionality, monitor market trends, experiment and iterate, collaborate with other developers, and future-proof your app. By following these strategies, you can ensure that your app remains relevant and meets the evolving needs of your users. In the next chapter, we will explore methods for protecting your no code app and users' data.

Chapter 18: Protecting Your No Code App and Users' Data

In today's digital age, data security and user privacy are paramount concerns for any application or platform. Regardless of whether you are using code or building a no code app, it is essential to prioritize the protection of your app and users' data. In this chapter, we will explore the key strategies and best practices for safeguarding your no code app and ensuring the security and privacy of your users' information.

UNDERSTANDING THE IMPORTANCE OF APP SECURITY

App security goes beyond simply protecting the codebase of your app. It encompasses various aspects, including data security, encryption, user authentication, secure data transfer, and protection against potential vulnerabilities and cyber threats. By prioritizing app security, you demonstrate your commitment to safeguarding user information, maintaining their trust, and complying with privacy regulations.

CHOOSING A SECURE NO CODE PLATFORM

When selecting a no code platform, it is crucial to consider the security measures they have in place. Look for platforms that offer robust security features such as data encryption, secure data storage, and regular security updates. Additionally, ensure that the platform complies with industry standards and regulations, such as GDPR (General Data Protection Regulation) or CCPA (California Consumer Privacy Act), depending on your target audience and geography.

SECURE DATA STORAGE AND ENCRYPTION

One of the fundamental steps in protecting your users' data is implementing secure data storage and encryption techniques. Most no code platforms provide built-in security features that allow you to store user data in a secure manner. Ensure that sensitive user information, such as passwords or payment details, is encrypted using strong encryption algorithms.

USER AUTHENTICATION AND ACCESS CONTROL

Implementing user authentication and access control mechanisms adds an extra layer of security to your no code app. Require users to create strong passwords and consider implementing additional authentication methods, such as two-factor authentication (2FA) or biometric authentication. Additionally, utilize role-based access control to restrict access to sensitive areas of your app only to authorized users.

REGULAR SECURITY UPDATES AND PATCHES

No code platforms often release regular updates and patches to address security vulnerabilities and improve the overall security of their platforms. Stay vigilant and ensure that your app is always up to date with the latest patches and security updates provided by the platform. Regularly check for available updates and apply them promptly to minimize the risk of security breaches.

THOROUGH TESTING FOR SECURITY VULNERABILITIES

Conducting thorough security testing is essential for identifying any potential vulnerabilities or weaknesses in your no code app. Perform penetration testing and vulnerability assessments to assess the resilience of your app against potential attacks. Also, ensure that any third-party integrations or plugins used in your app undergo rigorous security testing to prevent vulnerabilities from arising through these components.

SECURE DATA TRANSFER AND COMMUNICATION

When developing a no code app, it is essential to ensure that data is transferred securely between your app and any external servers or APIs. Use secure protocols, such as HTTPS, for data transfer and communication, which encrypts data in transit. Additionally, avoid transmitting user data in plain text and encrypt sensitive information during transmission.

USER CONSENT AND PRIVACY POLICIES

Obtaining user consent and communicating your privacy policies transparently is crucial for building user trust. Clearly explain to users how their data will be used, stored, and protected. Provide options for users to opt out or delete their data if they wish to do so. Ensure that your privacy policies are compliant with relevant regulations and always keep your users informed about any changes to your policies.

MONITORING AND INCIDENT RESPONSE

Implement continuous monitoring of your app's security to detect any suspicious activities or potential breaches promptly. Set up logging and monitoring systems to track and analyze app usage, detect anomalies, and respond to incidents effectively. Establish an incident response plan to mitigate potential risks and outline steps to be taken in the event of a security breach.

TRAINING AND AWARENESS

Invest in training and awareness programs for yourself and your team to stay updated on the latest security practices and best practices in app security. Regularly educate your team on security protocols, responsible handling of user data, and potential security risks. By fostering a culture of security awareness, you can minimize the likelihood of security incidents.

CONCLUSION

Protecting your no code app and users' data is an ongoing effort that requires proactive measures and continuous vigilance. By implementing robust security measures, choosing a secure no code platform, encrypting data, conducting thorough testing, and prioritizing user privacy, you can create a safe and trustworthy environment for your app and users. Always stay informed about emerging security threats and adapt your security practices accordingly to stay ahead of potential risks.

Chapter 19: Building a Strong Brand for Your No Code App

A strong brand is crucial for the success of any business, including your no code app. Building a brand helps differentiate your app from competitors, creates recognition and loyalty among users, and establishes credibility and trust in the market. In this chapter, we will explore the steps involved in building a strong brand for your no code app and discuss strategies for effective brand building.

DEFINING YOUR TARGET AUDIENCE

Before you can start building your brand, it's important to have a clear understanding of your target audience. Identify who your app is intended for and conduct thorough market research to gain insights into their needs, preferences, and behaviors. This knowledge will help you tailor your brand message and design to resonate with your target audience.

CONDUCTING MARKET RESEARCH

Market research plays a crucial role in brand building. Analyze the market landscape, identify your competitors, and evaluate their branding strategies. This will help you identify gaps and opportunities, allowing you to position your app uniquely in the market.

CREATING USER PERSONAS

User personas are fictional representations of your target audience, based on market research and data. They help you understand your users on a deeper level, enabling you to create a brand that speaks directly to their needs and desires. Develop user personas that reflect different segments of your target audience, and use them as a reference when making branding decisions.

CREATING A STRONG BRAND IDENTITY

Your brand identity is the visual and verbal representation of your app. It encompasses your app's name, logo, color scheme, typography, and tone of voice. Take time to craft a unique and memorable brand identity that aligns with your target audience's preferences and your app's purpose.

CHOOSING A BRAND NAME

Your app's name is a critical component of your brand identity. It should be memorable, easy to pronounce and spell, and reflective of your app's value proposition. Consider conducting trademark checks and domain name availability research to ensure your chosen name is legally viable.

DESIGNING A UNIQUE LOGO

A well-designed logo can instantly communicate your brand's personality and values. Invest in professional logo design or use no code design tools to create a unique and visually appealing logo that captures the essence of your app.

USING CONSISTENT BRANDING ELEMENTS

Consistency is key when it comes to building a strong brand. Use consistent branding elements across all touchpoints, including your app, website, social media profiles, and marketing materials. This includes ensuring consistent use of colors, typography, imagery, and tone of voice.

CRAFTING A COMPELLING BRAND STORY

A compelling brand story helps users connect with your brand on an emotional level. Craft a narrative that communicates your app's purpose, values, and unique selling points. Share your brand story through your app's website, social media content, and other marketing channels.

LEVERAGING DIFFERENT MARKETING CHANNELS

Once you have established your brand, it's important to promote it through various marketing channels. This includes incorporating App Store Optimization (ASO) techniques, content marketing, influencer marketing, email marketing, and paid advertising. Choose the marketing channels that align with your target audience's preferences and behaviors.

CONCLUSION

Building a strong brand for your no code app is essential for standing out in the market and attracting and retaining users. By defining your target audience, conducting market research, creating a strong brand identity, and leveraging different marketing channels, you can establish a brand that resonates with your audience and drives the success of your app.

Remember to continuously monitor and refine your brand strategy based on user feedback and market trends.

Chapter 20: Collaborating and Hiring Help for Your App

Collaboration and hiring help are essential steps in the development process of your app. Whether you're a solo entrepreneur or part of a team, working with others can bring tremendous value to your app and accelerate its success. In this chapter, we'll explore the importance of collaborating with others and provide guidance on hiring help for your app development journey.

THE POWER OF COLLABORATION

Collaboration is the key to unlocking innovation and creativity in your app development process. By involving others, you can benefit from their diverse perspectives, skills, and expertise. Here are some reasons why collaboration is crucial for your app's success:

1. Access to Different Skill Sets

When collaborating with others, you have the opportunity to work with individuals who possess skills that complement your own. For example, if you have a strong design background but lack technical programming skills, collaborating with a developer can help you bring your design ideas to life. By leveraging the strengths of others, you can create a well-rounded app that meets the needs of your target audience.

2. Increased Productivity and Efficiency

Collaboration allows tasks to be divided and conquered, leading to increased productivity and efficiency. By working as a team, you can leverage the strengths of each team member and streamline the development process. This division of labor can help you accomplish more in less time and meet deadlines effectively.

3. Diverse Perspectives and Ideas

When you collaborate with others, you open yourself up to a world of diverse perspectives and ideas. Each team member brings their unique experiences and insights, which can lead to innovative solutions and approaches. By tapping into this collective wisdom, you can ensure that your app meets the needs of a broader audience and stands out from the competition.

4. Reduced Risk

Collaboration can help mitigate risks associated with app development. When you work with others, you can identify potential pitfalls and challenges early on, allowing you to address them proactively. Additionally, the collective expertise of the team can help you navigate through uncertainties and make informed decisions, minimizing the chances of costly mistakes.

HIRING HELP FOR YOUR APP

While collaboration is essential, there may come a point where you need to hire external help to support your app development journey. Whether it's hiring freelancers, consultants, or a development agency, here are some considerations to keep in mind:

1. Define Your App Requirements

Before hiring help, it's crucial to have a clear understanding of your app's requirements. Define the features, functionalities, and scope of your app to communicate your needs effectively to potential collaborators or hires. Having a detailed app brief or project plan can help you attract the right talent and ensure everyone is aligned on the project goals.

2. Evaluate Skills and Expertise

When hiring external help, thoroughly evaluate the skills and expertise of potential collaborators or hires. Look for individuals or agencies with relevant experience in app development, preferably within your industry or niche. Review their portfolios or case studies to assess the quality of their work and determine if they align with your vision for the app.

3. Check References and Reviews

Before finalizing any collaboration or hire, check references and reviews from previous clients or employers. This due diligence can help you gain insights into their work ethics, communication skills, and ability to meet deadlines. Reach out to their past clients and ask about their experience working with the individual or agency.

4. Establish Clear Expectations and Contracts

When hiring external help, it's crucial to establish clear expectations and outline the terms of the collaboration or contract. Clearly communicate the deliverables, timelines, and payment structure to avoid any misunderstandings or conflicts down the line. Consider drafting a formal agreement or contract that protects both parties' rights and specifies the scope of the project.

5. Communication and Project Management

Effective communication and project management are key to successful collaboration. Establish channels of communication that suit all parties involved, whether it's email, project management tools, or virtual meetings. Regularly communicate updates, progress, and feedback to ensure that everyone is on the same page. Consider using project management tools to track tasks, set deadlines, and monitor the progress of the project.

6. Foster a Positive Working Relationship

Building a positive working relationship is essential for successful collaboration. Treat your collaborators or hires with respect, trust their expertise, and provide constructive feedback. Encourage open communication and create a collaborative environment that fosters creativity and innovation. Recognize and appreciate the contributions of your collaborators, as it will motivate them to go above and beyond in delivering the best possible outcome.

CONCLUSION AND NEXT STEPS

Collaboration and hiring help can take your app development journey to new heights. By leveraging the strengths and expertise of others, you can accelerate the success of your app and create a high-quality product that meets the needs of your target audience. Remember to define your app requirements, evaluate skills and expertise, establish clear expectations, foster effective communication, and nurture positive working relationships. With the right collaborators and hires, your app will have the potential to thrive in the competitive app market.

Chapter 21: The Importance of Customer Support and Communication

UNDERSTANDING THE VALUE OF CUSTOMER SUPPORT

Providing excellent customer support plays a crucial role in the success of any app, including those built with no code. Customer support goes beyond just resolving technical issues; it encompasses building relationships, addressing user concerns, and ensuring overall satisfaction. Here, we will explore the reasons why customer support is essential for the growth and longevity of your app.

Building Trust and Loyalty

Effective customer support helps build trust and loyalty among users. When users know that there is a reliable support system in place, they feel more confident in using your app and are more likely to recommend it to others. By addressing their concerns promptly and professionally, you can create a positive experience that fosters trust and establishes a loyal user base.

Improving User Retention

Customer support plays a pivotal role in user retention. When users encounter issues or have questions, timely and efficient support can help resolve their concerns, preventing them from abandoning your app.

By providing swift resolutions and personalized assistance, you can enhance the user experience and increase the likelihood of user retention.

Gathering User Feedback and Insights

An effective customer support system allows you to gather valuable insights and feedback from your users. By actively listening to their concerns and suggestions, you can identify areas for improvement and make data-driven decisions to enhance your app. This feedback can also help you uncover new features, identify usability issues, and pinpoint areas of your app that may require further optimization.

Enhancing User Satisfaction

Prompt and effective customer support contributes to overall user satisfaction. When users receive the necessary support to resolve their issues, they feel valued and appreciated. This positive experience leads to higher user satisfaction, which in turn increases the chances of positive app reviews, referrals, and future engagement.

BEST PRACTICES FOR CUSTOMER SUPPORT AND COMMUNICATION

To ensure a successful customer support system for your no code app, consider implementing the following best practices:

Establish Multiple Support Channels

Offer various channels for users to reach out to you, such as email, live chat, social media, and a dedicated support portal. This allows users to choose the channel they are most comfortable with and increases the chances of prompt assistance.

Provide Clear and Updated Documentation

Create comprehensive documentation, including FAQs, user guides, and troubleshooting resources. Make sure they are easily accessible and regularly updated to address common issues and provide self-help options for users.

Train and Empower Customer Support Representatives

Invest in training your customer support representatives to ensure they have deep knowledge of your app and can effectively address user issues. Empower them with the authority to make decisions and resolve problems independently, reducing the need for unnecessary escalations.

Be Proactive in Anticipating User Needs

Take a proactive approach to address potential user concerns and questions.

Monitor user feedback, app reviews, and social media mentions to identify recurring issues and provide preemptive solutions or guidance.

Personalize the Support Experience

Treat each user as an individual by personalizing your support interactions. Use their name in communications, refer to previous interactions, and demonstrate empathy and understanding. Personalization can greatly enhance the user experience and foster a stronger connection with your app.

Monitor and Respond to Feedback

Regularly monitor user feedback, app reviews, and social media mentions. Respond promptly and professionally to both positive and negative feedback, showing users that you value their opinions and are committed to continuous improvement.

Implement a Feedback and Bug Reporting System

Provide users with an easy and convenient way to submit feedback and bug reports directly within your app. This not only encourages users to provide feedback but also streamlines the process of collecting and managing user input.

CONCLUSION: PRIORITIZING CUSTOMER SUPPORT AND COMMUNICATION

Customer support and effective communication are essential for the success of your no code app. By prioritizing the needs of your users, offering timely and efficient support, and actively seeking their feedback, you can significantly enhance the user experience, build trust and loyalty, and ultimately drive the success and growth of your app. Remember that customer support is not just a means to resolve issues but also an opportunity to engage with your users, gather insights, and continuously improve your app.

Chapter 22: Expanding Your App to Global Markets

Expanding your app to global markets opens up new opportunities for growth and success. With the rise of the digital age, reaching users worldwide has become easier than ever before. However, entering international markets requires careful planning, localization, and cultural sensitivity. In this chapter, we will explore the steps and strategies involved in expanding your app to global markets.

UNDERSTANDING THE GLOBAL MARKET LANDSCAPE

Before venturing into new international markets, it is important to conduct thorough market research and analysis.

Understanding the global market landscape will help you identify potential opportunities and challenges. Here are a few key factors to consider: 1. Market Demand: Research the demand for your app in different countries or regions. Identify markets with a high potential user base and a need for your app's offerings. 2. Competition: Analyze the competitive landscape in each market. Identify existing players, their market share, and their strategies. Determine how your app can differentiate itself and provide unique value to users. 3. Cultural and Legal Considerations: Research and understand the cultural, legal, and regulatory norms of each target market. Ensure that your app complies with local laws and regulations, and tailor your marketing and content to align with cultural sensitivities. 4. Market Trends: Stay updated on the latest market trends, consumer behavior, and technology adoption rates in each target market. This will help you adapt your app and marketing strategies accordingly.

LOCALIZATION AND INTERNATIONALIZATION

Localization and internationalization are crucial steps in expanding your app to global markets. Localization involves adapting your app to the language, culture, and preferences of your target audience, while internationalization refers to designing and developing your app to be easily adaptable to different languages and regions. Here are some key considerations for localization and internationalization: 1. Language: Translate your app's content, including user interface elements, text, and multimedia assets, into the local language. Use professional translation services or work with native speakers to ensure accuracy and cultural appropriateness. 2. Date and Time Formats: Adapt date and time formats, measurement units, and currency symbols to align with the local conventions of your target market. 3. Cultural Sensitivity: Avoid any content,

151

imagery, or symbols that may be offensive or misinterpreted in the local culture. Be mindful of local customs, holidays, and taboos when designing your app's user experience. 4. User Experience: Optimize the user experience for different markets. Consider factors such as internet connectivity, device specifications, and user preferences when designing your app's features and functionality.

MARKETING AND LOCALIZATION STRATEGIES

Marketing plays a crucial role in expanding your app to global markets. Tailor your marketing strategies to each target market to maximize your reach and impact. Here are some effective strategies to consider: 1. Localized App Store Optimization (ASO): Optimize your app's metadata, keywords, and descriptions in each target market's app store. Use localized screenshots, videos, and app previews to showcase your app's features and benefits. 2. Localization

Testing: Conduct thorough testing of your app's localized versions before launching in each market. Ensure that all text, images, and features are properly adapted and functional. 3. Influencer Partnerships: Collaborate with influencers who have a strong presence in your target markets. They can help promote your app, increase brand awareness, and attract new users. 4. Localized Content Marketing: Create localized blog posts, articles, videos, and social media content to engage users in each target market. Tailor your content to address local interests, trends, and pain points. 5. Paid Advertising: Invest in targeted advertising campaigns in each target market. Use platforms such as Google Ads, social media advertising, and local ad networks to reach your desired audience. 6. Localization of Customer Support: Provide customer support in the local language of your target markets. This will ensure a seamless user experience and help address any concerns or issues promptly.

USER FEEDBACK AND ITERATION

Expanding to global markets requires continuous learning and adaptation. Pay close attention to user feedback from different markets and iterate your app accordingly. Here's how you can effectively gather and utilize user feedback: 1. Feedback Channels: Provide multiple channels for users to submit feedback, such as in-app feedback forms, email, or social media. Encourage users to provide suggestions, report bugs, and share their experiences. 2. Localization Feedback: Pay particular attention to feedback from users in different markets. Understand their specific needs, preferences, and pain points. Use this feedback to improve your app's localization and user experience. 3. Iterative Development: Continuously update and refine your app based on user feedback and market trends. Release regular updates to address bug fixes, add new features, and improve overall user satisfaction. 4. Monitoring App Store Reviews: Regularly monitor and respond to user reviews on app stores in different markets. Address any concerns or issues promptly and maintain a positive relationship with your users. By implementing these strategies, you can successfully expand your app to global markets and tap into new user bases. Remember to adapt your app, content, and marketing efforts to align with the preferences and cultural sensitivities of each target market. Continuously gather user feedback and iterate your app to ensure long-term success and user satisfaction.

Chapter 23: Utilizing SEO and ASO to Increase App Visibility

In today's competitive app market, simply building a great app is not enough. To ensure your app reaches the right audience and stands out from the crowd, you need to employ effective strategies to increase its visibility. Two key strategies for achieving this are Search Engine Optimization (SEO) and App Store Optimization (ASO). By understanding and implementing these techniques, you can significantly improve your app's discoverability and attract more users.

UNDERSTANDING SEO

SEO is the practice of optimizing your app's online presence to improve its ranking in search engine results. While SEO techniques are commonly associated with websites, they can also be applied to mobile apps. The goal of SEO is to increase organic traffic to your app's website or landing page, which in turn can lead to more app downloads. Here are some key elements to consider when implementing SEO for your app: 1.

Keyword Research:

Research and identify relevant keywords that are commonly used by your target audience when searching for apps. Use tools like Google Keyword Planner or other keyword research tools to identify high-volume, low-competition keywords. 2.

Optimized App Content:

Incorporate your target keywords into your app's title, description, and other relevant metadata. Make sure your app's content is clear, concise, and provides a compelling description of what your app offers. 3.

Backlinks and External Promotion:

Build backlinks to your app's website or landing page from reputable sources to increase your app's authority and visibility. Engage in external promotion through online communities, forums, and social media platforms to generate buzz and drive traffic to your app. 4.

App Reviews and Ratings:

Positive reviews and ratings can significantly impact your app's visibility. Encourage satisfied users to leave reviews and ratings, and promptly address any negative feedback to maintain a positive reputation. 5.

Mobile-Friendly Website:

Ensure your app's website or landing page is optimized for mobile devices. A responsive and user-friendly website will not only enhance the user experience but also improve your app's search engine ranking.

UNDERSTANDING ASO

ASO is the process of optimizing your app's metadata within app stores to improve its visibility in search results and increase its chances of being discovered by potential users. Similar to SEO, ASO involves various factors that influence your app's ranking and visibility within the app store. Here are some key elements to consider when implementing ASO for your app: 1.

App Title and Keywords:

Choose an app title that accurately reflects your app's purpose and includes relevant keywords. Incorporate keywords strategically throughout your app's description and metadata to improve its search relevancy. 2.

App Icon:

Design an eye-catching and memorable app icon that represents your app and captures the attention of potential users browsing the app store. 3.

App Screenshots and Videos:

Use high-quality screenshots and videos that showcase your app's features and benefits. Optimize these assets to provide a visual representation of your app's value, encouraging users to download it. 4.

App Ratings and Reviews:

Encourage satisfied users to rate and review your app. Positive ratings and reviews can improve your app's visibility and credibility, influencing the decision-making process of potential users. 5.

Localization:

Adapt your app's metadata and content to cater to different markets and languages. By localizing your app, you can increase its visibility in specific regions and attract users from diverse language backgrounds. 6.

Regular Updates:

Continuously update your app with bug fixes, feature enhancements, and new content. Regular updates not only improve user experience but also signal to app stores that your app is actively maintained and relevant.

MEASURING AND ITERATING

Both SEO and ASO are ongoing processes that require continuous monitoring, measurement, and iteration. Keep track of your app's performance in search engine rankings and app store rankings. Identify areas for improvement based on user feedback and analytics. Test different approaches to see what works best for your app, and adjust your strategies accordingly. Remember, the ultimate goal of utilizing SEO and ASO is to increase your app's visibility, drive organic traffic, and attract more users. By implementing these strategies effectively, you can improve your app's discoverability and maximize its chances of success in the competitive app market. Keep refining your SEO and ASO techniques to stay ahead of the competition and ensure your app reaches its full potential.

Chapter 24: Building a Community Around Your App

Building a community around your app is a key strategy for fostering user engagement, loyalty, and long-term success. A community provides a platform for users to connect with each other, share experiences, and provide valuable feedback. Furthermore, a strong community can serve as a valuable marketing tool, as satisfied users are likely to spread the word about your app to their networks. In this chapter, we will explore the steps involved in building a community around your app and maintaining an active and engaged user base.

UNDERSTANDING THE IMPORTANCE OF COMMUNITY

Before diving into the specifics of building a community, it is essential to understand why building a community is crucial for the success of your app. A community not only serves as a support network for your users but also creates a sense of belonging and ownership, fostering loyalty and trust. A vibrant community can also act as a promotional channel for your app, as enthusiastic users are likely to share their positive experiences with others. Additionally, a community can provide valuable insights and feedback that can help you improve and iterate your app based on real-world user needs.

CREATING A COMMUNITY PLATFORM

To build a community around your app, you need to establish a dedicated platform where users can connect and engage with each other. This platform could take the form of a forum, a social media group, a chat channel, or a combination of these. When choosing a platform, consider the preferences and behaviors of your target audience. For example, if your app caters to a tech-savvy audience, a forum or a Slack channel might be a suitable choice. On the other hand, if your app targets a broader demographic, a Facebook or LinkedIn group could work well.

FOSTERING ENGAGEMENT

Once you have established a community platform, the next step is to foster user engagement. Here are some strategies to encourage active participation and conversation among community members:

Provide Valuable Content

Share informative and relevant content with your community members, such as tutorials, tips and tricks, case studies, industry news, and updates about your app. This will keep your community engaged and provide them with valuable insights.

Encourage User-generated Content

Empower your community members to contribute their own content, such as success stories, testimonials, app customization examples, and feature suggestions. User-generated content not only provides valuable insights but also fosters a sense of ownership within the community.

Organize Events and Challenges

Organize events, challenges, or competitions within your community to encourage participation and foster a sense of fun and camaraderie. For example, you can host coding competitions, design challenges, or even virtual meetups and webinars.

Facilitate Discussions and Q&A Sessions

Encourage community members to ask questions, seek help, and share their expertise by facilitating regular discussions and Q&A sessions. This will not only create a supportive environment within the community but also provide an opportunity for users to learn from each other.

RECOGNIZING AND REWARDING COMMUNITY MEMBERS

Recognizing and rewarding active community members is essential for maintaining engagement and building a loyal user base. Consider implementing a system of badges, levels, or rewards that users can unlock based on their contributions to the community. This can include recognition for helping others, sharing valuable content, providing insightful feedback, or even just being an active and supportive member. Publicly acknowledging and highlighting community members' achievements can further incentivize engagement and foster a sense of pride within the community.

MONITORING AND MODERATING THE COMMUNITY

As the community grows, it is important to carefully monitor and moderate community interactions. Set clear community guidelines and rules to ensure a positive and inclusive environment. Regularly review and moderate community discussions to maintain a respectful and constructive atmosphere. Address any conflicts or issues promptly and impartially to prevent them from escalating.

USING COMMUNITY FEEDBACK TO IMPROVE YOUR APP

One of the most valuable aspects of having a community is the opportunity to gather feedback and insights to improve your app. Actively listen to your community members' suggestions, feature requests, and bug reports. Regularly solicit feedback and conduct surveys to gather insights on how to enhance user experience. Consider implementing a system for community members to vote or prioritize feature requests, allowing them to have a direct impact on the app's development roadmap.

CONCLUSION

Building a community around your app is a powerful strategy for fostering user engagement, loyalty, and long-term success. By creating a dedicated platform, fostering engagement, recognizing and rewarding community members, monitoring and moderating discussions, and using community feedback to iterate and improve your app, you can build a vibrant and supportive community that not only enhances the user experience but also serves as a promotional tool for your app. Continuously invest time and effort in building and nurturing your community to unlock the full potential of your app.

Chapter 25: Creating Engaging App Content

Creating engaging app content is crucial for capturing and retaining the attention of users. In today's digital age, content is not only king, but it also plays a vital role in establishing a strong brand identity and driving user engagement. In this chapter, we will explore strategies and best practices for creating compelling app content that resonates with your target audience and keeps them coming back for more.

UNDERSTANDING THE IMPORTANCE OF ENGAGING APP CONTENT

Engaging app content is the key to attracting and retaining users. Whether it's written text, images, videos, or interactive elements, the content you create for your app needs to be informative, entertaining, and valuable to your users. Here are a few reasons why engaging app content matters: 1. Capturing Attention: In today's fast-paced digital world, users have a limited attention span. Engaging content can capture their attention and entice them to explore your app further. 2. Building Trust and Credibility: High-quality and valuable content helps build trust and credibility with your users. When you consistently deliver valuable content, users are more likely to trust your brand and become loyal advocates. 3. Driving User Engagement: Engaging content encourages users to interact with your app, whether it's leaving comments, sharing content with their social networks, or taking part in interactive experiences within the app. These engagements can drive user retention and increase app usage. 4. Enhancing User Experience: Well-crafted content contributes to an overall positive user experience. By providing helpful and relevant information, you can guide users through your app and ensure they have a seamless and enjoyable experience.

BEST PRACTICES FOR CREATING ENGAGING APP CONTENT

Now that we understand the importance of engaging app content, let's explore some best practices for creating content that captivates your users: 1. Know Your Audience: Before you start creating content, it's essential to understand your target audience. Conduct market research, create user personas, and identify their needs, preferences, and pain points. This knowledge will help you tailor your content to meet their specific needs effectively. 2. Create Valuable and Relevant Content: Your app content should provide value to your users. Whether it's educational, entertaining, or inspirational, ensure that the content you create resonates with your target audience. Use a mix of formats such as articles, videos, infographics, and podcasts to cater to different user preferences. 3. Maintain Consistency: Consistency is key when it comes to creating engaging app content. Establish a consistent tone of voice, branding elements, and visual style across all your content to create a cohesive and recognizable brand identity. Consistency also helps build trust and familiarity with your users. 4. Use Visuals to Enhance Content: Visuals play a crucial role in making your content engaging. Incorporate high-quality and relevant images, videos, and graphics to enhance the user experience. Visuals can capture attention, break up text, and convey information more effectively. 5. Incorporate Interactive Elements: Interactive elements, such as quizzes, polls, surveys, and interactive infographics, can significantly enhance user engagement. These elements not only make your content more interactive and fun but also encourage users to actively participate and share their opinions. 6. Optimize for Mobile: As more users access apps on mobile devices, it's crucial to optimize your content for mobile viewing. Ensure that your content is mobile-friendly, with responsive design, legible fonts, clear visuals, and easy navigation. Test your content on different devices and screen sizes to ensure a seamless experience. 7. Use SEO Techniques: Implementing basic search engine optimization (SEO) techniques can help your app content rank higher in search engine results. Conduct keyword research, optimize your headlines and descriptions, and include relevant keywords naturally throughout your content. 8. Encourage User-generated Content: User-generated content, such as reviews, comments, and user-generated posts, can add authenticity and create a sense of community within your app. Encourage users to share their experiences, feedback, and ideas to foster user engagement and create a user-centric app experience. 9. Leverage Personalization: Personalizing your app content based on user preferences and behaviors can significantly increase user engagement. Utilize user data to deliver personalized recommendations, targeted content, and personalized notifications to create a customized experience for each user. 10. Continuously Iterate and Improve: Creating engaging app content is an iterative process. Monitor user engagement metrics, gather user feedback, and analyze user behavior to understand what content performs well and what needs improvement. Use these insights to refine your content strategy and create even more compelling content.

CONCLUSION

Creating engaging app content is essential for capturing and retaining the attention of users. By understanding the importance of engaging content and implementing best practices, you can create content that resonates with your target audience, enhances user engagement, and drives the success of your app. Remember to know your audience, provide valuable and relevant content, maintain consistency, use visuals, incorporate interactive elements, optimize for mobile, leverage SEO techniques, encourage user-generated content, personalize content, and continuously iterate and improve. With these strategies in place, you can create an app with content that captivates and delights your users.

Chapter 26: Understanding App Store Guidelines and Policies

App stores, such as the Apple App Store and Google Play Store, have specific guidelines and policies that developers must adhere to in order to have their apps approved and listed. Understanding these guidelines and policies is crucial for a successful app launch and maintaining compliance with the app store's rules. In this chapter, we will explore the importance of understanding app store guidelines and policies, and provide tips on how to navigate these requirements effectively.

THE SIGNIFICANCE OF APP STORE GUIDELINES AND POLICIES

App store guidelines and policies serve several important purposes. Firstly, they help ensure that the app store maintains a high standard of quality, security, and user experience. By setting specific requirements, app stores strive to protect users from harmful or low-quality apps that may compromise their privacy or device stability. Secondly, app store guidelines and policies ensure fair competition among app developers. They provide a level playing field where all developers follow the same rules and have equal opportunities to present their apps to users. This helps create a trustworthy ecosystem where users can confidently discover and download apps. Lastly, app store guidelines and policies help app developers understand the best practices for app development and distribution. By following these guidelines, developers can ensure their apps meet the standards set by the app store, enhancing the chances of approval and success.

NAVIGATING APP STORE GUIDELINES AND POLICIES

To successfully navigate app store guidelines and policies, it is important to thoroughly review and understand them before starting the app development process. Here are some key steps to help you navigate these requirements effectively:

1. Read and Familiarize Yourself with the Guidelines

Start by reading and familiarizing yourself with the app store guidelines and policies. These guidelines are typically available on the app store's website or developer portal. Take the time to carefully go through each section and understand the specific requirements and recommendations.

2. Keep Abreast of Updates and Changes

App store guidelines and policies are regularly updated to adapt to changing technologies and market trends. It is important to stay informed about these updates and changes to ensure your app remains compliant. Subscribe to app store newsletters or developer blogs, join relevant forums or communities, and follow official social media accounts to stay updated on any policy changes.

3. Incorporate Guidelines into the App Development Process

As you plan and develop your app, consider the app store guidelines and policies from the beginning. Design and implement features and functionalities that align with these guidelines to reduce the chances of rejection during the review process. This includes adhering to UI design guidelines, privacy and data security requirements, content restrictions, and any specific app category guidelines.

4. Test and Optimize for App Store Compliance

Before submitting your app for review, thoroughly test it to ensure it meets the app store guidelines and policies. Test all functionalities, check for any content that may violate the guidelines, and assess the app's performance and stability. Consider using testing tools provided by the app store or third-party services to ensure compliance.

5. Prepare and Submit a Comprehensive App Store Listing

When submitting your app for review, ensure that your app store listing provides all the necessary information and assets according to the guidelines. This includes a clear app description, relevant screenshots and videos, accurate categorization, and compliance with app metadata requirements. Provide any additional documentation or permissions needed for specific functionalities, such as accessing user data or implementing in-app purchases.

6. Respond to Feedback and Appeals

In some cases, your app may not meet all the guidelines initially and may receive feedback or be rejected during the review process. Take this feedback as an opportunity to improve your app and address any issues or concerns raised by the app store. Make the necessary updates and resubmit your app for review. If your app is rejected or faces any issues with compliance, you may have the option to appeal the decision or seek clarification from the app store's support team. Follow the established procedures and provide any additional information or evidence to support your case.

CONCLUSION

Understanding app store guidelines and policies is essential for successfully navigating the app review process and ensuring compliance with the rules set by the app store. By familiarizing yourself with these guidelines, incorporating them into your app development process, and staying updated on any changes, you can increase the chances of having your app approved and reaching your target audience. Remember to continuously monitor and iterate your app to maintain compliance with evolving guidelines and policies.

Chapter 27: Leveraging Artificial Intelligence in No Code Apps

Artificial Intelligence (AI) has become a transformative technology in various industries, and its integration in no code app development brings new possibilities and capabilities. AI enables apps to automate tasks, analyze data, make predictions, and provide personalized experiences. In this chapter, we will explore how you can leverage AI in your no code apps to enhance functionality and deliver a better user experience.

THE ROLE OF ARTIFICIAL INTELLIGENCE IN NO CODE APPS

Artificial Intelligence can be integrated into no code apps in various ways, including:

1. Natural Language Processing (NLP)

NLP allows apps to understand and interpret human language. By incorporating NLP capabilities, your app can analyze user inputs, extract meaning from text, and generate appropriate responses. This opens up opportunities for building chatbots, virtual assistants, and language translation features without complex coding.

2. Machine Learning (ML)

Machine Learning algorithms enable apps to automatically learn from data and improve their performance over time. ML models can be trained to recognize patterns, classify data, make predictions, and recommend personalized content or actions. Without having to write code, you can leverage ML platforms to create intelligent features such as product recommendations, content personalization, and fraud detection.

3. Computer Vision

Computer Vision allows apps to process and interpret visual information. Through image recognition, object detection, and optical character recognition (OCR), your app can analyze images, extract relevant information, and perform actions based on what it "sees". This opens up possibilities for building apps that can recognize faces, identify objects, or extract text from images without complex coding.

4. Sentiment Analysis

Sentiment Analysis uses AI to analyze and extract the sentiment or emotion behind text data, such as social media posts or customer reviews. By integrating sentiment analysis into your app, you can gain insights into user opinions, feedback, and sentiment trends. This can help you understand user satisfaction, identify areas of improvement, and provide targeted responses or actions accordingly.

5. Predictive Analytics

Predictive Analytics leverages AI to forecast future outcomes based on historical data. By analyzing patterns, trends, and relationships within data, your app can make predictions or recommendations. This can be applied in various contexts, such as sales forecasting, inventory optimization, or personalized recommendations. No code platforms with built-in predictive analytics capabilities allow you to harness the power of AI without writing complex algorithms.

BENEFITS OF LEVERAGING AI IN NO CODE APPS

Integrating AI into your no code apps offers several benefits, including:

1. Automation of Routine Tasks

AI can automate repetitive and mundane tasks, freeing up time and resources for more important activities. By automating tasks like data entry, content moderation, or customer support, your app can improve efficiency and reduce manual effort.

2. Improved User Engagement and Experience

AI-powered features can enhance the user experience by offering personalized recommendations, tailored content, or intelligent search. By understanding user preferences and behaviors, your app can deliver relevant and engaging experiences, leading to increased user satisfaction and retention.

3. Enhanced Decision Making

With AI-driven analytics and insights, your app can provide valuable information to assist in decision-making processes. By analyzing data, identifying patterns, and predicting outcomes, your app can offer valuable insights and recommendations to users, enabling them to make more informed decisions.

4. Scalability and Adaptability

AI algorithms and models can learn and adapt to changing circumstances, allowing your app to scale and evolve over time. This flexibility enables your app to handle increasing data volumes, user demands, and new scenarios without extensive coding efforts.

INTEGRATING AI IN NO CODE APPS

To leverage AI in your no code apps, you can take advantage of AI-focused features and integrations provided by no code platforms. These platforms often offer drag-and-drop interfaces, pre-built AI models, or easy-to-use AI development tools. By exploring the capabilities of these platforms, you can incorporate AI functionality into your app without the need for extensive coding knowledge. When integrating AI into your no code app, consider the following steps:

1. Identify AI Use Cases

Determine how AI can add value to your app by identifying use cases that align with your goals and target audience. Whether it's language translation, sentiment analysis, image recognition, or predictive analytics, understanding your app's requirements will help you select the most suitable AI features.

2. Choose the Right AI Tools

Research and evaluate the available AI tools and platforms that align with your app's requirements and your level of expertise. Consider factors such as ease of use, customization options, integration capabilities, scalability, and support. Select a tool that enables you to leverage AI functionality while aligning with your app's overall development strategy.

3. Implement AI Functionality

Once you have chosen the right AI tool, follow the platform's documentation and guidelines to integrate AI functionality into your no code app. This may involve configuring API connections, training AI models with your data, or utilizing pre-built AI components available on the platform. Test and iterate on the AI functionality to ensure it meets your app's requirements and provides the desired user experience.

4. Monitor and Refine

Continuously monitor the AI functionality within your app, collecting data and feedback to evaluate its performance. Analyze the effectiveness of the AI features and iterate based on user feedback and insights. This iterative approach will help you refine the AI functionality, ensuring that it remains effective and aligned with user expectations.

CONCLUSION

Artificial Intelligence offers exciting opportunities for enhancing the functionality and user experience in no code apps. By leveraging AI capabilities such as Natural Language Processing, Machine Learning, Computer Vision, Sentiment Analysis, and Predictive Analytics, app creators can deliver personalized, intelligent, and engaging experiences to their users. By exploring the AI features and integrations provided by no code platforms, you can harness the power of AI without the need for extensive coding knowledge. Incorporate AI functionality strategically into your no code apps, and continuously monitor and refine it based on user feedback and market trends.

Chapter 28: Harnessing the Power of Automation in No Code Apps

Automation plays a crucial role in today's fast-paced digital landscape. It enables businesses to streamline processes, increase efficiency, and focus on value-added tasks. In the context of no code apps, automation can revolutionize the way you develop, deploy, and manage your applications.

THE BENEFITS OF AUTOMATION IN NO CODE APPS

Automation offers several key benefits for no code app development: **1. Saves Time and Effort:** By automating repetitive and time-consuming tasks, you can free up valuable time and resources. This allows you to focus on more critical aspects of your app, such as user experience and innovation. **2. Enhances Efficiency:** With automation, you can streamline workflows and eliminate manual errors. This improves overall efficiency and helps deliver a high-quality app in less time. **3. Increases Scalability:** Automation allows you to scale your app without the need for extensive coding. This means you can easily handle a growing user base and adapt to changing market demands. **4. Improves Accuracy:** Manual tasks are prone to errors, but automation ensures consistency and accuracy in the app development process. This leads to a more reliable and robust product. 5. **Enables Integration:** Automation allows for seamless integration with other tools and services. This enables you to leverage the power of APIs and third-party services, expanding the functionalities of your app. 6. **Reduces Costs:** By automating tasks, you can significantly reduce costs associated with manual labor and human errors. This makes app development more cost-effective, especially for small businesses and startups with limited budgets.

AREAS OF AUTOMATION IN NO CODE APPS

Automation can be applied to various aspects of no code app development. Here are some key areas where automation can make a difference: 1. **Deployment and Version Control:** Automation can simplify the deployment process by automatically building, testing, and deploying your app to various platforms. It can also help manage version control, ensuring that updates and bug fixes are efficiently implemented. 2. **Data Management:** Automation can assist in handling data from different sources and integrating it into your app. It can automatically fetch, transform, and update data, ensuring real-time accuracy and reliability. 3. **User Onboarding:** Automation can streamline the user onboarding process by automatically sending welcome emails, creating user accounts, and guiding new users through the app's features and functionalities. 4. **User Engagement:** Automation can be utilized to send personalized push notifications, triggered emails, and in-app messages to engage and retain users. These automated communications can be tailored based on user behavior, preferences, and milestones. 5. **Reporting and Analytics:** Automation can generate regular reports and provide real-time analytics about app usage, user behavior, and performance metrics. This allows you to make data-driven decisions and continuously optimize your app. 6. **Customer Support:** Automation can provide automated responses to common user queries and efficiently route support tickets to the appropriate team members. It can also automate the process of collecting user feedback and suggestions.

IMPLEMENTING AUTOMATION IN NO CODE APPS

To harness the power of automation in your no code app, consider the following steps: 1. **Identify Tasks to Automate:** Assess your app development process and identify tasks that can be automated. Look for repetitive, time-consuming, and error-prone tasks that can benefit from automation. 2. **Choose the Right Automation Tools:** Explore the available automation tools and services that integrate with your chosen no code platform. Look for tools that align with your specific automation needs and provide seamless integration. 3. **Map Out Automation Workflows:** Create a visual representation of your app development process, highlighting the tasks that will be automated. Define the inputs, outputs, and triggers for each automated task. 4. **Implement Automation:** Configure the automation tools and services based on the workflows defined in the previous step. Test and validate the automation to ensure it functions as intended. 5. **Monitor and Iterate:** Continuously monitor the performance and efficiency of your automated processes. Collect feedback from users and stakeholders to identify areas for improvement and iterate on your automation workflows.

CASE STUDIES OF SUCCESSFUL AUTOMATION IN NO CODE APPS

To better understand the impact of automation in no code apps, let's explore a couple of case studies: 1. **Case Study 1: E-commerce App** - Automation is used to import product information, update inventory, and process orders in real-time from various suppliers. - Automated email notifications are sent to customers at different stages of the order fulfillment process. - AI-powered chatbots handle customer inquiries and provide personalized recommendations based on user preferences and shopping history. 2. **Case Study 2: Fitness Tracking App** - Automation is used to integrate with wearable devices, automatically sync user data, and provide real-time fitness statistics. - Push notifications are sent automatically to remind users about their workout schedules and congratulate them on achieving milestones. - Automated reports and analytics provide users with insights into their progress and help them set new fitness goals.

CONCLUSION

Automation is a game-changer in no code app development. By harnessing the power of automation, you can save time, increase efficiency, improve accuracy, and enhance the overall user experience. Consider the different areas of automation discussed in this chapter and start exploring automation tools and services that align with your app's needs. Continuously iterate on your automation workflows to stay ahead in the evolving landscape of no code app development.

INTRODUCTION

Integrating Application Programming Interfaces (APIs) and web services into your no code app can greatly enhance its functionality and provide access to a wide range of services and data. APIs allow different software applications to communicate and exchange information, enabling your app to leverage external resources and deliver a more robust experience to your users.

UNDERSTANDING APIS AND WEB SERVICES

What are APIs?

APIs, or Application Programming Interfaces, are sets of rules and protocols that allow different software applications to communicate and interact with each other. They define a specific set of functionalities and data structures that developers can utilize to access certain features or services provided by another application or system.

What are Web Services?

Web services are a type of API that utilize web-based technologies to enable communication between different software applications over the internet. Web services provide a standardized way for applications to exchange data and perform specific functions, such as retrieving information from a database or performing a calculation.

BENEFITS OF API AND WEB SERVICE INTEGRATION

Integrating APIs and web services into your no code app offers several benefits: 1. Enhanced Functionality: By integrating APIs and web services, you can access features and services that are not natively available in your app. This allows you to expand the capabilities of your app and provide additional value to your users. 2. Time and Cost Savings: Instead of building complex functionalities from scratch, you can leverage existing APIs and web services to quickly add desired features to your app. This saves development time and reduces costs associated with custom development. 3. Seamless Integration: APIs and web services provide well-defined interfaces and protocols, making it easier to integrate them into your app. This ensures smooth communication between your app and external services, resulting in a seamless user experience. 4. Access to External Data:

APIs and web services often provide access to external data sources, such as weather data, location information, or social media feeds. By integrating these services, your app can provide real-time and relevant information to users. 5. Scalability and Flexibility: APIs and web services are designed to handle high volumes of requests and can scale with your app's growth. They also provide flexibility for future updates and enhancements, as you can easily replace or update the integrated services without changing the core functionality of your app.

CHOOSING AND INTEGRATING APIS

When choosing APIs and web services to integrate into your no code app, consider the following factors: 1. Compatibility: Ensure that the API or web service you select is compatible with the no code platform you are using. Check for any restrictions or limitations imposed by the platform on integrating external services. 2.

Functionality: Evaluate the functionality and features provided by the API or web service. Make sure it aligns with the needs and goals of your app, and that it enhances the user experience. 3. Reliability and Support: Research the reputation and reliability of the API or web service provider. Look for documentation, developer support, and community forums to ensure you can address any issues that may arise during integration. 4. Scalability: Consider the scalability of the API or web service. Ensure it can handle increased traffic and user demand as your app grows. 5. Security: Evaluate the security measures taken by the API or web service provider to protect user data. Ensure that the integration does not compromise the security of your app or the privacy of your users. Once you have chosen the APIs or web services to integrate, you can begin the integration process. The specific steps will depend on the no code platform you are using, but generally, it involves the following: 1. Obtaining API Keys or Credentials: Most

APIs and web services require authentication for accessing their resources. Obtain the necessary API keys or credentials from the service provider. 2. Setting Up API Integration: Depending on the no code platform, you may need to configure the API integration settings. This includes providing the API keys or credentials and specifying the desired endpoints or functionalities to integrate. 3. Testing and Troubleshooting: Test the API integration to ensure that it functions correctly. Validate that data is being retrieved or pushed as expected and troubleshoot any errors or issues that may arise. 4. Monitoring and Maintenance: Once the API integration is live, continuously monitor the integration to ensure its ongoing reliability. Stay alert for any updates or changes to the API or web service that may require adjustments to your integration.

USE CASES FOR API AND WEB SERVICE INTEGRATION

API and web service integration can be applied in various use cases to enhance the functionality of your no code app. Some examples include: 1. Payment Gateway Integration: Integrate a payment gateway API to enable in-app purchases or subscription models in your app, offering a seamless and secure payment experience for users. 2. Geolocation Integration: Integrate a geolocation API to provide location-based services in your app, such as displaying nearby points of interest or personalized recommendations based on the user's location. 3. Social Media Integration: Integrate social media APIs to allow users to log in with their social media accounts, share content from your app, or access social media feeds directly within your app. 4. Email Service Integration: Integrate an email service API to send automated emails, such as welcome emails, notifications, or updates to users, fostering communication and engagement. 5. External Data Integration: Integrate APIs that provide access to external data sources, such as weather data, financial data, or news feeds, to enrich your app's content and functionality.

CONCLUSION

Integrating APIs and web services into your no code app offers numerous benefits, including enhanced functionality, time and cost savings, seamless integration, access to external data, and scalability. By carefully selecting and integrating these services, you can create a more robust and dynamic app that meets the needs and expectations of your users. Remember to consider compatibility, functionality, reliability, scalability, and security when choosing APIs and web services, and follow the necessary steps for integration, testing, and ongoing maintenance.

Chapter 30: The Future of No Code Development

The future of no code development is filled with exciting possibilities and potential. As technology continues to evolve, so does the no code movement, opening doors for individuals to create powerful and innovative applications without the need for traditional coding skills. One of the trends that we can expect to see in the future of no code development is the continued growth and expansion of no code platforms. These platforms will become more advanced and sophisticated, offering a wider range of tools and features to empower users in building their applications. As technology advances, we can anticipate the introduction of new and cutting-edge capabilities, such as artificial intelligence and machine learning integrations, voice recognition, augmented reality, and virtual reality functionalities into these platforms. With the increasing demand for mobile applications, the future of no code development will also prioritize mobile-first design and development. No code platforms will continue to enhance their mobile app development capabilities, enabling users to create highly responsive and user-friendly mobile applications. This will allow individuals to tap into the growing market of mobile users and provide engaging experiences on smartphones and tablets. Another area that the future of no code development will focus on is collaboration and community building. No code platforms will provide more opportunities for users to collaborate with each other, share resources, and learn from one another. This could include features like user forums, online communities, and marketplace platforms that allow users to exchange ideas, templates, and components. By fostering collaboration, no code development will become more inclusive and encourage the sharing of knowledge and expertise. As the no code movement continues to gain momentum, it is also likely that we will see an increase in the number of niche-specific no code platforms. These platforms will cater to specific industries or use cases, offering specialized tools and functionalities tailored to the unique needs of those domains. This will empower individuals within these industries to create customized solutions that address their specific challenges and requirements. One of the most exciting aspects of the future of no code development is the potential for democratized software development. No code platforms will continue to break down barriers and make app development accessible to a wider audience. This will empower individuals from diverse backgrounds and industries to bring their ideas to life, without the need for extensive coding knowledge or technical expertise. This democratization of software development will lead to a more inclusive and diverse app ecosystem, with a greater variety of applications catering to a wider range of needs. In conclusion, the future of no code development is full of possibilities. With advancements in technology and the continued growth of the no code movement, individuals will have even more tools and resources at their disposal to create innovative, user-friendly, and powerful applications. Collaboration, mobile-first design, niche-specific platforms, and the democratization of software development will shape the future of no code, unlocking new opportunities and empowering individuals to become creators in the digital world. As this exciting future unfolds, the potential for individuals to shape the technology landscape and bring their ideas to life has never been greater.

Chapter 31: Case Studies of Successful No Code Apps

In this chapter, we will explore several case studies of successful no code apps that have made a significant impact in their respective industries. These case studies will provide valuable insights into how different entrepreneurs and businesses have leveraged the power of no code development to create innovative and successful applications. By examining their strategies, challenges, and achievements, we can gain inspiration and learn valuable lessons for our own app development journeys.

CASE STUDY 1: FITNESS TRACKING APP

Our first case study explores a fitness tracking app that was developed using a no code platform. This app aimed to help users track their daily physical activities, set fitness goals, and monitor their progress over time. The key features of this app included real-time activity tracking, personalized workout plans, and data visualization for easy interpretation of fitness metrics. The development team chose a no code platform that offered customizable templates and a drag-and-drop interface. This allowed them to quickly build and iterate the app without the need for complex coding. They also integrated various APIs to enable real-time activity tracking by connecting with popular fitness wearables. To ensure a successful launch, the team conducted thorough market research to understand the target audience's preferences and pain points. They identified the need for a user-friendly interface, seamless integration with popular fitness devices, and personalized workout recommendations. Based on this research, they designed the app's UI/UX with simplicity, intuitive navigation, and visually appealing data visualization. To acquire users, the team focused on content marketing by creating informative blog posts and videos related to fitness and wellness. They also collaborated with fitness influencers on social media to create buzz and increase brand awareness. User engagement was further enhanced through gamification features like challenges, achievements, and a social community within the app. The fitness tracking app received positive feedback from users, who appreciated the simplicity, accuracy, and personalized features it offered. With continuous iteration based on user feedback and market trends, the app grew its user base and generated revenue through in-app purchases of premium workout plans and ad partnerships with fitness-related brands.

CASE STUDY 2: E-COMMERCE APP

Our second case study delves into an e-commerce app that allowed users to browse and purchase a wide range of products from multiple vendors. The app aimed to provide a seamless shopping experience and increase customer engagement and retention. The development team opted for a no code platform that offered the flexibility to integrate with various vendor APIs, manage product listings, and handle secure payment transactions. They utilized the platform's drag-and-drop interface to design the app's layout, product pages, and shopping cart functionalities. To create a strong brand presence, the team focused on creating a unique and visually appealing app design. They carefully curated product listings, optimized product images, and implemented user-friendly filters and search options. They also leveraged social media platforms to promote products, collaborate with influencers, and encourage user-generated content through contests and giveaways. To retain customers and provide exceptional customer support, the team implemented a live chat feature within the app. This allowed users to ask questions, seek assistance, and receive timely responses from customer support representatives. They also gathered user feedback through in-app surveys and reviews and continuously optimized the app based on this feedback. The e-commerce app gained popularity due to its user-friendly interface, extensive product selection, and efficient customer support. By offering exclusive discounts and loyalty rewards, the app successfully retained customers and encouraged repeat purchases. The team also implemented personalized product recommendations, further enhancing user engagement and driving sales.

CASE STUDY 3: FOOD DELIVERY APP

Our third case study explores a food delivery app that revolutionized the way people order food from their favorite restaurants. The app aimed to provide a seamless and convenient platform for users to discover nearby restaurants, browse menus, place orders, and track deliveries in real-time. The development team chose a no code platform that offered extensive customization options and integrations with popular food delivery APIs and payment gateways. This allowed them to create a seamless user experience by enabling features like real-time order tracking, secure payment options, and personalized recommendations. To ensure a successful app launch, the team collaborated with local restaurants to onboard them onto the platform. They offered incentives such as waived commission fees for a limited period and provided training and support to help restaurants optimize their menus and manage orders efficiently. To acquire users, the team utilized a multifaceted marketing strategy. They implemented app store optimization techniques to improve app visibility and rankings. They also partnered with influential food bloggers and vloggers to create engaging content and drive user acquisition through referral links and promotional campaigns. Additionally, they utilized social media platforms to showcase mouth-watering food images, share customer testimonials, and run targeted ads. The food delivery app gained popularity due to its intuitive user interface, wide range of restaurant choices, and seamless order and delivery experience. By continuously refining their app based on user feedback and market trends, the team further improved customer satisfaction and retention. The app generated revenue through commissions on orders and partnerships with restaurants for featured listings and promotional campaigns.

CONCLUSION

These case studies highlight the immense potential of no code development in creating successful and innovative applications. By leveraging the power of no code platforms, entrepreneurs and businesses can overcome traditional coding barriers and bring their ideas to life faster and more cost-effectively. The key takeaways from these case studies include the importance of understanding the target audience, designing intuitive user interfaces, integrating relevant APIs, implementing effective marketing strategies, gathering user feedback for continuous improvement, and staying agile in a dynamic market. As you embark on your own no code app development journey, these case studies serve as a valuable source of inspiration and guidance. By learning from the successes and challenges faced by others, you can enhance your app's chances of achieving remarkable success in your chosen industry.

Chapter 32: Common Mistakes and How to Avoid Them

INTRODUCTION

When it comes to building and launching a no code app, there are common mistakes that many developers make. These mistakes can lead to wasted time, resources, and missed opportunities. It's important to understand these pitfalls and learn how to avoid them in order to increase the chances of app success. In this chapter, we will explore some of the most common mistakes in no code app development and provide strategies for avoiding them.

MISTAKE 1: LACK OF PROPER PLANNING

One of the biggest mistakes in no code app development is jumping into the project without proper planning. Rushing into development without a clear understanding of the app's purpose, target audience, and desired features can lead to a disorganized and ineffective app. To avoid this mistake, take the time to define your app's goals, identify the target audience, and outline the key features and functionalities before starting development.

Start by conducting market research to understand the needs and preferences of your potential users. This will help you tailor your app to their specific requirements. Create user personas to visualize your target audience and their goals. Use this information to inform your app's design, functionality, and user experience. By thoroughly planning your app before development, you can ensure that it aligns with your objectives and meets the needs of your target audience.

MISTAKE 2: OVERCOMPLICATING THE USER INTERFACE

Another common mistake in no code app development is overcomplicating the user interface (UI). The UI plays a crucial role in the success of your app as it determines how users interact with it. If the UI is cluttered, confusing, or difficult to navigate, users are likely to become frustrated and abandon your app. Therefore, it's important to keep the UI simple, intuitive, and user-friendly.

When designing the UI for your app, prioritize simplicity and ease of use. Use consistent design elements, intuitive navigation, and clear labeling. Avoid overcrowding the screen with too many features or options. Instead, focus on the core features and functionalities that provide the most value to your users. Conduct usability testing with real users to gather feedback and identify areas for improvement. By keeping the UI clean and user-friendly, you can enhance the overall user experience and increase user satisfaction.

MISTAKE 3: NEGLECTING USER TESTING

One of the most critical mistakes in no code app development is neglecting user testing. User testing involves gathering feedback from real users to identify usability issues, uncover bugs, and gather insights for improvement. By skipping this step, you miss out on valuable feedback that can help you optimize your app and enhance its user experience.

To avoid this mistake, incorporate user testing throughout the development process. Start by conducting usability testing with a small group of target users to evaluate the app's ease of use, navigation, and overall user experience. Gather feedback and make iterative improvements based on the insights gained from testing. Additionally, consider beta testing your app with a larger group of users to gather feedback on a wider scale.

Implementing user feedback is crucial for creating a user-centered app that meets the needs and expectations of your target audience. It allows you to address any issues or concerns early on and make necessary refinements before launching your app to the wider audience.

MISTAKE 4: IGNORING PERFORMANCE OPTIMIZATION

Performance optimization is often overlooked in no code app development. However, neglecting to optimize your app's performance can lead to slow loading times, crashes, and a poor user experience. Users expect fast and responsive apps, and if your app fails to meet these expectations, they may look for alternatives.

To avoid this mistake, prioritize performance optimization from the start. Optimize your app's code by removing unnecessary elements, compressing files, and minifying code. Optimize images and multimedia to reduce file sizes without sacrificing quality. Implement caching mechanisms to reduce server load and improve app loading times. Regularly conduct performance testing to identify and address any bottlenecks or areas for improvement.

Consider scalability as well. As your app grows and attracts more users, you need to ensure that it can handle increased traffic and demand without sacrificing performance. Use load balancing techniques and scalable infrastructure to accommodate growing user numbers. By prioritizing performance optimization, you create a faster and more efficient app that provides a seamless user experience.

MISTAKE 5: FAILURE TO ITERATE AND IMPROVE

A common mistake in no code app development is failing to iterate and improve on the app's initial version. Building an app is an ongoing process, and user needs and market trends are constantly evolving. If you fail to iterate and improve your app over time, it may become outdated, lose relevance, and fail to meet the changing expectations of your users.

To avoid this mistake, embrace an iterative mindset and continuously seek feedback and insights from your users. Monitor user behavior, analyze app metrics, and pay attention to user feedback to identify areas for improvement. Regularly release updates that address user needs and provide added value. Stay updated with the latest trends and technologies in the no code development space and incorporate them into your app when appropriate.

By continuously iterating and improving your app, you demonstrate your commitment to delivering a high-quality product and provide ongoing value to your users. This helps you stay competitive in the market and retain and attract new users.

CONCLUSION

Avoiding common mistakes in no code app development is crucial for building a successful and effective app. By taking the time to plan your app, simplify the UI, conduct user testing, optimize performance, and continuously iterate and improve, you can increase the chances of app success and create a valuable product for your target audience.

Chapter 33: Handling App Feedback and Negative Reviews

User feedback and reviews are valuable sources of insights and opportunities for improvement in app development. However, not all feedback will be positive, and negative reviews can have a significant impact on the reputation and success of your app. In this chapter, we will explore strategies for effectively handling app feedback and negative reviews, turning them into opportunities for growth and improvement.

WHY APP FEEDBACK IS IMPORTANT

Feedback from users provides valuable insights into their experiences and perceptions of your app. It can help you identify usability issues, bugs, and areas for improvement. App feedback allows you to understand user needs and expectations, helping you make informed decisions for future updates. By actively listening to user feedback, you can enhance the user experience, increase user retention, and boost app ratings and reviews.

ESTABLISHING FEEDBACK CHANNELS

To effectively handle app feedback, it is essential to establish clear and easily accessible feedback channels. This could include in-app feedback forms, surveys, email addresses, or social media platforms where users can reach out to provide their feedback. By providing multiple feedback channels, you increase the chances of gathering valuable insights from a diverse range of users.

RESPONDING PROMPTLY AND PROFESSIONALLY

When users take the time to provide feedback, it is crucial to acknowledge their efforts promptly. Responding to feedback shows that you value their input and are committed to improving the app. Whether the feedback is positive or negative, always respond professionally and maintain a courteous tone. Address the user's concerns or questions and provide helpful information or solutions.

TURNING NEGATIVE FEEDBACK INTO OPPORTUNITIES

Negative reviews can be challenging to handle, but they can also present valuable opportunities for growth and improvement. Instead of getting defensive or ignoring negative feedback, use it as a chance to learn and iterate. Look for common themes or patterns in the negative feedback and identify areas that need improvement. Develop a plan to address these issues, and communicate your plans to users, showcasing your commitment to their satisfaction.

ENCOURAGING AND SHOWCASING POSITIVE FEEDBACK

Positive feedback from users is just as important as negative feedback. It serves as validation for your hard work and can help build a positive reputation for your app. Encourage users to share their positive experiences by providing incentives, such as discounts, rewards, or exclusive features. Showcase positive feedback on your app's website or social media platforms to boost user confidence and attract new users.

MONITORING APP STORE REVIEWS

App store reviews are a crucial aspect of user feedback. Monitor app store reviews regularly and respond to both positive and negative reviews. Engage with users by thanking them for positive reviews and addressing their concerns in negative reviews. By actively participating in app store discussions, you demonstrate your dedication to providing a quality user experience.

ITERATING BASED ON USER FEEDBACK

Continuously gather feedback and analyze it to inform your next development cycle. Use user feedback to prioritize new features, enhance existing features, or fix bugs and issues. Consider implementing A/B testing to validate proposed changes based on user feedback and data. By iterating based on user feedback, you can create an app that better meets the needs and expectations of your target audience.

CONCLUSION

App feedback and reviews are valuable sources of insights for app improvement and user satisfaction. By establishing clear feedback channels, responding promptly and professionally, and embracing both positive and negative feedback, you can create a feedback-driven development process that leads to a better app.

Continuously iterate based on user feedback to create an app that not only meets user expectations but exceeds them.

Chapter 34: Scaling Your App for Growth

Scaling your app for growth is a critical step in the development process, as it ensures that your app can handle increased traffic and user demand without sacrificing performance. Scaling involves designing and implementing strategies to accommodate growth and maintain a seamless user experience.

UNDERSTANDING THE IMPORTANCE OF SCALING

As your app gains popularity and attracts more users, it is essential to scale your infrastructure, databases, and resources to meet the increasing demand. Failure to scale adequately can result in slow app performance, crashes, and frustrated users, leading to negative reviews and a decline in user retention. Scaling your app is not just about increasing server capacity; it involves optimizing your code, databases, and caching mechanisms to handle the growing user base effectively. Scalability is crucial for ensuring that your app remains responsive, reliable, and available, regardless of the number of users and transactions.

SCALING TECHNIQUES FOR NO CODE APPS

1.

Horizontal Scaling:

In horizontal scaling, you add more servers or instances to distribute the workload across multiple machines. This approach allows your app to handle increased traffic by adding more resources. Horizontal scaling is particularly beneficial for handling sudden spikes in traffic and ensuring high availability. 2.

Vertical Scaling:

Vertical scaling involves upgrading your existing servers or infrastructure to handle more substantial workloads. This approach focuses on increasing the capacity of individual servers or instances. Vertical scaling is suitable for apps that require high processing power or specific hardware configurations. 3.

Load Balancing:

Load balancing distributes incoming network traffic across multiple servers to effectively manage the workload. This technique helps prevent server overload and ensures that each server operates within its optimal capacity. Load balancing can be implemented using built-in features provided by your chosen no code platform or by integrating third-party load balancing services. 4.

Caching:

Caching involves storing frequently accessed data in a cache, such as in-memory databases or content delivery networks (CDNs). By caching data, you can reduce the number of requests made to your server and improve app performance. Caching not only enhances the user experience but also relieves the backend resources, allowing your app to handle more users efficiently. 5.

Database Optimization:

As your app scales, the demands on your database increase. Optimizing your database involves techniques such as indexing, query optimization, database partitioning, and sharding. These techniques help improve database performance, reduce response times, and ensure that the database can handle increasing data loads.

MONITORING AND TESTING

Monitoring and testing are crucial during the scaling process to ensure that your app is performing optimally and can handle increased traffic. Here are some strategies to consider: 1.

Performance Monitoring:

Implement tools and services to monitor your app's performance, including response times, server resources utilization, database performance, and user experience metrics. Continuous monitoring helps detect bottlenecks and identifies areas that require optimization. 2.

Load Testing:

Perform load testing to simulate heavy traffic and measure how your app performs under stress. Load testing identifies potential performance issues, scalability limitations, and areas where additional resources or optimizations are needed. 3.

Data Backup and Recovery:

As your app scales, ensuring data integrity and availability becomes crucial. Implement robust backup and recovery mechanisms to protect user data and reduce downtime in the event of a failure.

ITERATIVE IMPROVEMENT AND FUTURE PLANNING

Scaling your app is an ongoing process, and it requires continuous iteration and improvement. Regularly analyze user feedback, conduct performance audits, and monitor market trends to identify areas for enhancement. As technology evolves, stay updated with the latest advancements in no code platforms and scalability strategies to adapt your app accordingly. When planning for future growth, consider factors such as market demand, user expectations, and potential feature enhancements. Continuously refine your app's scalability plans to align with your long-term goals and ensure that your app can handle exponential growth.

CONCLUSION

Scaling your app for growth is crucial for its long-term success. By understanding the importance of scaling, implementing scaling techniques, monitoring and testing performance, and planning for future growth, you can ensure that your app can handle increased user demand without sacrificing performance or user experience. Continuous iteration and improvement are key to maintaining a scalable and successful no code app.

Chapter 35: Building a Sustainable Business around Your No Code App

In this chapter, we will explore the steps and strategies required to build a sustainable business around your no code app. While developing a successful app is an accomplishment in itself, creating a sustainable business model is crucial for long-term growth and profitability.

UNDERSTANDING THE IMPORTANCE OF A SUSTAINABLE BUSINESS MODEL

A sustainable business model ensures that your app can generate consistent revenue and maintain a competitive advantage in the market. It involves identifying the target market, understanding customer needs, and implementing effective monetization strategies. Here are some key benefits of building a sustainable business model for your no code app: 1. Revenue Generation: A sustainable business model allows you to generate revenue consistently, ensuring financial stability and growth. This revenue can be reinvested into further development, marketing, and customer acquisition. 2. Scalability: A sustainable business model enables your app to scale and handle increased user demand without sacrificing performance. It ensures that your infrastructure, resources, and processes can support growth and expansion. 3. Competitive Advantage: Building a sustainable business model helps you stand out from the competition. By continuously improving your app and addressing customer needs, you can differentiate yourself in the market and attract a loyal customer base. 4. Longevity: A sustainable business model ensures the long-term viability of your app. It allows you to adapt to changes in technology, user preferences, and market trends, ensuring that your app remains relevant and profitable.

IDENTIFYING YOUR TARGET MARKET

To build a sustainable business around your no code app, it's important to clearly identify your target market. Understanding your target audience's needs, preferences, and pain points will help you develop a product that resonates with them. Here are some steps to identify your target market: 1. Conduct Market Research: Research your industry and competition to understand market trends, customer preferences, and potential gaps in the market. This will help you identify opportunities for your app. 2. Define Customer Personas: Create detailed profiles of your ideal customers, including demographics, behaviors, preferences, and goals. This will help you tailor your app's features, design, and marketing strategies to meet their needs. 3. Gather User Feedback: Engage with your target audience through surveys, interviews, and beta testing. This will provide valuable insights into their preferences, pain points, and expectations, allowing you to refine your app and business model.

SELECTING THE RIGHT MONETIZATION STRATEGY

Monetization is a key aspect of building a sustainable business around your no code app. Choosing the right monetization strategy depends on your app's target audience, features, value proposition, and competition. Here are some popular monetization strategies for no code apps: 1. Freemium: Offer a basic version of your app for free, but charge for premium features or additional content. This allows users to experience the app before committing to a purchase. 2. In-App Purchases: Sell virtual goods, premium content, or additional functionality within your app. This strategy works well for apps with a strong focus on user engagement and customization. 3. Subscriptions: Offer users access to premium features or content on a recurring basis. This strategy is suitable for apps that provide ongoing value and regular updates. 4. Advertising: Display ads within your app and generate revenue through ad impressions or clicks. Consider the user experience and ensure that ads are relevant and non-intrusive. 5. Affiliate Marketing: Partner with relevant businesses and earn a commission for referring users who make a purchase. This strategy works well when your app aligns with specific industries or products. 6. Sponsorship: Collaborate with brands or businesses to promote their products or services within your app. This can be done through sponsored content, in-app branding, or exclusive offers. It's important to evaluate each monetization strategy based on factors such as your target audience's preferences, competitors' strategies, and market trends. You can also experiment with different strategies and iterate based on user feedback and performance metrics.

OPTIMIZING USER ACQUISITION AND RETENTION

User acquisition and retention are critical for the success of your no code app and your sustainable business. Here are some strategies to optimize user acquisition and retention: 1. App Store Optimization (ASO): Optimize your app's listing in app stores by using relevant keywords, compelling descriptions, appealing visuals, and positive user reviews. This will improve your app's visibility and attract organic traffic. 2. Content Marketing: Create high-quality content, such as blog posts, tutorials, case studies, and videos, to educate and engage your target audience. Share this content on your website, social media platforms, and relevant communities to attract and retain users. 3. Influencer Marketing: Collaborate with influencers or industry experts to promote your app. Their endorsement and reach can help expand your app's visibility, credibility, and user base. 4. Email Marketing: Build an email list and send personalized, targeted emails to engage users, share updates, and offer exclusive promotions. Regular communication will help nurture relationships and encourage repeat app usage. 5. Gamification: Incorporate gamification elements into your app, such as rewards, achievements, and leaderboards, to drive user engagement and retention. Encourage users to compete, interact, and share their progress with others. 6. Push Notifications: Use push notifications strategically to engage and re-engage users. Send personalized messages, updates, and offers based on user behavior and preferences to keep them coming back to your app. 7. Regular Updates and Bug Fixes: Continuously improve your app by releasing updates and bug fixes. This shows users that you are actively maintaining and enhancing your app, increasing user trust and satisfaction. 8. Customer Support and Communication: Provide prompt and helpful customer support through multiple channels, such as in-app chat, email, and social media. Actively listen to user feedback, address their concerns, and communicate updates and improvements. Remember, user acquisition and retention are ongoing processes that require attention and continuous refinement. By consistently improving your app, addressing user needs, and delivering value, you can create a loyal user base and build a sustainable business.

CONCLUSION: CREATING A SUSTAINABLE BUSINESS AROUND YOUR NO CODE APP

Building a sustainable business around your no code app is essential for long-term success and profitability. By understanding your target market, selecting the right monetization strategy, optimizing user acquisition and retention, and continuously improving your app, you can create a strong foundation for your business. Remember to gather user feedback, monitor market trends, and adapt your strategies and offerings accordingly. Building a sustainable business requires ongoing effort, agility, and a deep understanding of your target audience. With commitment and strategic planning, you can create a successful and sustainable business around your no code app.

Chapter 36: Exploring Advanced Features and Capabilities

In the ever-evolving world of no-code development, it's important to stay up-to-date with the latest advancements in technology and explore advanced features and capabilities offered by no-code platforms. By harnessing these advanced features, you can take your no-code app to the next level and build innovative and unique solutions.

1. AI-POWERED FUNCTIONALITY

Artificial Intelligence (AI) has become a game-changer in various industries, and it can also be integrated into no-code apps to add intelligent and personalized functionality. No-code platforms are now offering pre-built AI models and integrations that enable you to easily incorporate AI capabilities into your app without the need for complex coding. With AI, you can empower your app with features such as natural language processing for chatbots and voice assistants, image recognition for enhanced visual experiences, predictive analytics to make data-driven decisions, and recommendation engines to provide personalized suggestions to users. These advanced AI-driven features can significantly enhance the user experience of your no-code app.

2. AUTOMATION AND WORKFLOW MANAGEMENT

Automation is a key aspect of no-code development that can greatly streamline processes and improve efficiency. No-code platforms now offer automation tools and workflow management capabilities that allow you to automate repetitive tasks, create customized workflows, and integrate with external services and APIs. By leveraging automation, you can automate data entry, notifications, email campaigns, and other routine tasks, saving time and reducing human error. This not only improves the efficiency of your app but also enhances the overall user experience by providing seamless and timely interactions.

3. DATABASE MANAGEMENT AND INTEGRATION

No-code platforms provide robust database management systems that enable you to store, organize, and retrieve data efficiently. These databases can handle complex data structures, allowing you to build sophisticated apps without the need for extensive coding. Furthermore, no-code platforms offer seamless integration with external databases and APIs, enabling you to retrieve and update data from various sources. This integration capability opens up a world of possibilities for your app, allowing you to leverage external data sources and services to enhance functionality and provide a richer user experience.

4. CUSTOM CODE INTEGRATION

While the focus of no-code development is to minimize or eliminate the need for traditional coding, there may be cases where you need to incorporate custom code to achieve specific functionalities. No-code platforms now provide the flexibility to integrate custom code snippets or scripts into your app, allowing you to extend the capabilities of your app beyond what the visual interface offers. This custom code integration feature enables you to tap into the vast ecosystem of libraries, frameworks, and APIs available in the coding world. It gives you the freedom to incorporate advanced functionalities, perform complex calculations, access low-level system features, and integrate with external services that are not readily available in the no-code platform.

5. REAL-TIME COLLABORATION

Collaboration is an essential aspect of app development, and no-code platforms are now offering real-time collaboration features that enable multiple users to work together on the same app simultaneously. This collaborative environment allows for efficient communication, seamless teamwork, and faster development cycles. Real-time collaboration features enable you to invite team members, assign tasks, and track progress, all within the no-code platform. It eliminates the need for back-and-forth communication through emails or other external tools, streamlining the development process and ensuring everyone is on the same page.

6. GAMIFICATION AND USER ENGAGEMENT

Gamification has proven to be a powerful tool for user engagement and retention. No-code platforms now offer built-in gamification features and components that enable you to integrate game-like elements into your app without the need for complex coding. With gamification, you can reward users for completing certain tasks or achieving specific milestones, stimulate competition through leaderboards, and provide interactive challenges and quizzes. These gamified experiences enhance user engagement, encourage user retention, and create a sense of enjoyment and accomplishment within your app.

7. AUGMENTED REALITY (AR) AND VIRTUAL REALITY (VR)

Augmented Reality (AR) and Virtual Reality (VR) technologies have gained significant popularity and are now accessible even to no-code developers. No-code platforms are incorporating AR and VR capabilities, allowing you to create immersive and interactive experiences within your app. By integrating AR and VR features, you can provide users with unique experiences, such as virtual tours, product visualizations, interactive 3D models, and virtual events. These advanced technologies add a new dimension to your app, ensuring it stands out in the crowded app market and captures the attention of users.

CONCLUSION

As the field of no-code development continues to evolve, exploring advanced features and capabilities offered by no-code platforms becomes crucial for building innovative and competitive apps. By incorporating AI-powered functionality, leveraging automation and workflow management, integrating databases and external services, incorporating custom code, enabling real-time collaboration, implementing gamification and user engagement, and integrating AR and VR, you can create unique, powerful, and user-centric applications. Stay ahead of the curve and take full advantage of the advanced features and capabilities provided by no-code platforms to unlock the full potential of your app.

Chapter 37: Customizing the User Experience in No Code Apps

The user experience (UX) plays a crucial role in the success of any app, including those built using no code platforms. While these platforms provide pre-designed templates and components to simplify the app development process, customizing the user experience is essential to create a unique and engaging app that meets the specific needs of your target audience. Here are some key considerations for customizing the user experience in your no code app:

1. UNDERSTAND YOUR TARGET AUDIENCE

Before customizing the user experience, it's important to have a deep understanding of your target audience. Conduct thorough market research, analyze user demographics, and gather insights into their preferences, behaviors, and pain points. This information will guide your decisions on how to tailor the app's UX to effectively meet the needs and expectations of your users.

2. DEFINE CLEAR USER FLOWS

Creating clear user flows is essential for a smooth and intuitive user experience. Map out the different actions and steps users will take within your app, and design logical and intuitive paths for them to follow. This includes determining the main features and functions of your app and how users will navigate through them.

3. DESIGN A CONSISTENT AND INTUITIVE INTERFACE

Consistency is key when it comes to creating a custom user experience. Users should be able to easily navigate your app and understand how to interact with different elements. Use consistent branding elements, such as colors, fonts, and icons, throughout the app to create a cohesive and recognizable interface. Additionally, prioritize simplicity and clarity in your design, ensuring that buttons, menus, and other interactive elements are intuitive and easy to understand.

4. PERSONALIZE THE USER EXPERIENCE

Personalization is a powerful way to engage users and make them feel valued. Leverage user data to provide personalized recommendations, suggestions, and content based on their preferences and behavior within the app. This could include personalized product recommendations, customized search results, or tailored notifications. By making the user experience feel more personalized, you can enhance user engagement and satisfaction.

5. OPTIMIZE FOR MOBILE DEVICES

With the increasing popularity of mobile devices, it's crucial to optimize your app for different screen sizes and mobile platforms. No code platforms often provide responsive design capabilities, allowing you to create a user experience that adapts seamlessly to smartphones and tablets. Test your app on various devices and screen resolutions to ensure that the user interface remains user-friendly and functional across different platforms.

6. LEVERAGE ANIMATION AND MICROINTERACTIONS

Animation and microinteractions can greatly enhance the user experience by adding visual interest and interactivity. Utilize subtle animations for transitions, loading indicators, and feedback messages to make the app feel more dynamic and responsive. Microinteractions, such as button animations or subtle haptic feedback, can provide users with a sense of control and delight.

7. IMPLEMENT ACCESSIBILITY FEATURES

Accessibility is an important aspect of customizing the user experience in your app. Consider the needs of users with disabilities and ensure that your app is inclusive and accessible to all. This may include providing alternative text for images, implementing screen reader compatibility, adjusting font sizes, and incorporating color contrast options. By making your app accessible, you can expand your user base and create a more inclusive experience.

8. CONTINUOUSLY GATHER USER FEEDBACK

To truly customize the user experience, it's important to gather user feedback throughout the development process. Implement feedback mechanisms, such as in-app surveys or feedback forms, to collect insights from your users. Take their suggestions and preferences into account when making updates and improvements to your app's UX. By involving your users in the customization process, you can create an app that truly meets their needs and expectations. In conclusion, customizing the user experience in no code apps is essential for creating a unique and engaging app that resonates with your target audience. By understanding your users, designing clear user flows, creating a consistent and intuitive interface, personalizing the experience, optimizing for mobile, leveraging animation and microinteractions, implementing accessibility features, and continuously gathering user feedback, you can create a user experience that stands out and drives the success of your no code app.

Chapter 38: Strategies for App Store Optimization (ASO)

App Store Optimization (ASO) is a crucial aspect of promoting and maximizing the visibility of your no code app in the app stores. ASO focuses on optimizing your app's metadata and content to increase its ranking in the app store search results, attract more organic downloads, and ultimately drive user acquisition. In this chapter, we will explore various strategies for effective ASO and provide practical tips to help you improve your app's visibility and increase downloads.

THE IMPORTANCE OF APP STORE OPTIMIZATION (ASO)

ASO plays a vital role in making your app discoverable and attracting potential users. With millions of apps available in the app stores, optimizing your app's presence becomes crucial to stand out from the competition. Here are some key reasons why ASO is essential: 1. Increased Visibility: ASO helps improve your app's ranking in the search results, ensuring it appears in relevant searches and increasing its discoverability. 2. Higher Organic Downloads: By optimizing your app's metadata, you can attract more organic traffic and increase the number of downloads without relying heavily on paid marketing campaigns. 3. Enhanced User Experience: ASO focuses on improving your app's user experience by optimizing the app's content, visuals, and user reviews, making it more appealing and trustworthy to potential users. 4. Cost-Effective

Marketing: ASO is a cost-effective strategy compared to other paid marketing channels, as it primarily relies on optimizing your app's metadata and content.

UNDERSTANDING THE ASO KEY FACTORS

To effectively optimize your app for the app stores, it's crucial to understand the key factors that influence ASO. These factors include: 1. App Title: The app title should be concise, descriptive, and contain relevant keywords. It should accurately represent your app's functionalities and value proposition. 2. App Keywords: Research and select relevant keywords that your target audience is likely to use when searching for an app similar to yours. Include these keywords in your app's title, subtitle, and keyword field. 3. App Description: Craft an engaging and informative app description that highlights the key features, benefits, and unique selling points of your app. Incorporate relevant keywords naturally to improve the app's searchability. 4. App Icon: Design an eye-catching and memorable app icon that represents your app's brand and purpose. A visually appealing icon can attract users' attention and drive clicks. 5. App Screenshots and Videos: Use high-quality screenshots and videos that showcase your app's user interface, features, and benefits. Visual content plays a crucial role in converting potential users into actual downloads. 6. App Ratings and Reviews: Encourage users to provide positive app ratings and reviews. Positive ratings and reviews increase your app's credibility and influence potential users' decisions. 7. Localization: Consider localizing your app's metadata, including the title, description, and keywords, to cater to international markets. Localized content increases the app's accessibility and discoverability in different regions.

BEST PRACTICES FOR ASO

Now that you understand the importance of ASO and the key factors that influence it, here are some best practices to help you optimize your app for the app stores: 1. Conduct Keyword Research: Use keyword research tools and analyze your competitors to identify relevant keywords with high search volume and low competition. Incorporate these keywords naturally into your app's metadata. 2. Optimize App Title: Make sure your app title is concise, unique, and keyword-rich. Include the most important keywords at the beginning of the title to improve search rankings. 3. Craft Compelling App Description: Write an engaging and informative app description that clearly communicates the value proposition of your app. Use bullet points, headers, and whitespace to enhance readability. 4. Use Eye-Catching Visuals: Design visually appealing app icons, screenshots, and videos that accurately represent your app's features and functionalities. Use clear and high-resolution images to create a positive impression. 5. Encourage Positive Ratings and Reviews: Implement strategies to encourage satisfied users to leave positive ratings and reviews. Respond promptly to user feedback and address any concerns or issues raised by users. 6. Analyze and Iterate: Continuously monitor your app's ASO performance using app analytics tools. Analyze the impact of your ASO strategies and iterate based on user feedback, trends, and competitor analysis. 7. Test and Optimize: A/B test different variations of your app's metadata, visuals, and conversion elements to identify the most effective optimizations. Continuously optimize your ASO strategy to achieve better results.

CONCLUSION

App Store Optimization (ASO) is a critical component of app marketing and can significantly impact the visibility and success of your no code app. By optimizing your app's metadata, visuals, and user engagement elements, you can increase its ranking in the app store search results, attract more organic downloads, and ultimately drive user acquisition. Implementing effective ASO strategies, conducting thorough keyword research, and continuously analyzing and iterating your app's ASO performance will help you stay ahead of the competition and maximize the potential of your no code app.

Chapter 39: Staying Motivated and Overcoming Challenges

Motivation is crucial for success in any endeavor, including no code app development. Building an app requires time, effort, and dedication, and it's natural to experience challenges and setbacks along the way. In this chapter, we will explore strategies to stay motivated and overcome the obstacles that may arise during the development process.

1. SET CLEAR GOALS

Setting clear goals provides a sense of direction and purpose. Start by defining your long-term vision for your app and break it down into smaller, achievable goals. Having a clear roadmap will help you stay focused and motivated when faced with challenges.

2. CELEBRATE SMALL WINS

Acknowledging and celebrating small wins along the way can boost motivation and provide a sense of accomplishment. As you reach milestones or make progress in your app development journey, take the time to acknowledge your achievements. This can be as simple as treating yourself to something you enjoy or sharing your progress with others.

3. SEEK SUPPORT AND ACCOUNTABILITY

Surround yourself with a supportive network of like-minded individuals who understand the challenges of app development. Join online communities, attend meetups, or engage with fellow app developers on social media platforms. Having a support system can provide encouragement, advice, and accountability when faced with challenges.

4. EMBRACE CONTINUOUS LEARNING

Every challenge is an opportunity to learn and grow. Stay curious and embrace a growth mindset. Seek out resources such as online courses, tutorials, and books to expand your knowledge and skills. Challenge yourself to explore new technologies, features, and trends in the world of no code development.

5. TAKE BREAKS AND PRACTICE SELF-CARE

Building an app can be mentally and physically demanding. It's important to take breaks and practice self-care to avoid burnout. Set aside time for relaxation, exercise, and hobbies outside of app development. Incorporate activities that help you recharge and reset your mind, such as mindfulness exercises or spending time in nature.

6. STAY POSITIVE AND LEARN FROM SETBACKS

Setbacks and challenges are inevitable in the app development process. Instead of getting discouraged, view them as opportunities for growth. Adopt a positive mindset and focus on learning from mistakes and finding solutions. Keep in mind that setbacks are often stepping stones to success and that persistence is key.

7. STAY UPDATED WITH INDUSTRY TRENDS

The world of app development is constantly evolving. Stay updated with the latest industry trends, new features, and advancements in no code platforms. This knowledge will not only keep you motivated but also allow you to stay ahead of the curve and leverage emerging technologies and techniques in your app.

8. CELEBRATE MILESTONES

In addition to celebrating small wins, it's important to celebrate major milestones in your app development journey. Completing major features, launching the app, or reaching a significant number of users are all milestones worth celebrating. Acknowledge your achievements and reflect on how far you've come.

9. SEEK FEEDBACK AND ITERATE

Seeking feedback from users and incorporating it into your app can be a source of motivation. User feedback provides valuable insights and shows that your app is making a positive impact. Embrace constructive criticism and iterate based on user suggestions to continuously improve your app.

10. REMEMBER YOUR WHY

When facing challenges, reminding yourself of why you started the app development journey can reignite your motivation. Reconnect with your passion, the problem you're solving, or the impact you want your app to make in the world. Keep your purpose in mind and let it drive you forward. Staying motivated and overcoming challenges is an essential part of the app development journey. By setting clear goals, celebrating wins, seeking support, continuous learning, practicing self-care, staying positive, staying updated with industry trends, celebrating milestones, seeking feedback, and remembering your why, you can maintain motivation and overcome obstacles that come your way. Stay resilient and committed to your vision, and success will follow.

Chapter 40: Conclusion and Next Steps

Congratulations! You have reached the end of this book, "The Only Book You Will Ever Need for Making Money with No Code." Throughout this journey, we have explored the exciting world of no code development and delved into various aspects of creating successful applications without traditional coding. No code development has revolutionized the software industry, empowering individuals without coding skills to unleash their creativity and bring their ideas to life. With no code platforms, the barriers to entry in app development have been lowered, making it accessible to a wider audience. By leveraging intuitive visual interfaces, drag-and-drop functionality, and pre-built components, anyone can design and build their own app. In this book, we have covered a wide range of topics, starting with understanding the no code movement and choosing the right platform for your app. We explored the process of building a Minimum Viable Product (MVP) and designing user-centered interfaces. We delved into testing and debugging techniques and the importance of integrating external services through APIs. We explored various monetization strategies, marketing and promotion techniques, and user acquisition and retention methods. We discussed the significance of analytics and data-driven decision making, as well as optimizing performance and scalability. We delved into designing for different devices and screen sizes, implementing in-app purchases and subscription models, leveraging social media, and utilizing push notifications to engage users. We also explored the importance of user feedback, adapting to changing technology and trends, protecting your app and users' data, building a strong brand, collaborating and hiring help, and the importance of customer support and communication. In the concluding chapter, let's take a moment to reflect on what we have learned and discuss the next steps you can take on your no code app development journey.

KEY TAKEAWAYS

Throughout this book, we have covered a vast array of topics related to no code app development. Here are some key takeaways: - No code development has democratized app development, making it accessible to individuals without coding skills. - No code platforms eliminate technical barriers and accelerate development, saving time and cost. -

Understanding the target audience and designing with user-centered principles greatly enhance the success of no code apps. - Testing and debugging are crucial steps in ensuring a seamless user experience and maintaining app quality. - Integrating external services and APIs can enhance the functionality of no code apps. - Implementing effective monetization strategies is essential for generating revenue. - Marketing and promotion play a vital role in acquiring users and increasing app visibility. - User acquisition and retention techniques are important for sustainable app growth. - Analytics and data-driven decision making provide valuable insights for app optimization. - Performance, scalability, and responsiveness are crucial for delivering an exceptional user experience. - Adapting to changing technology and trends ensures the longevity and relevance of your app. - Protecting your app and users' data is essential for maintaining trust and security. - Building a strong brand creates recognition, loyalty, and trust among your user base. - Collaboration and hiring help can accelerate the success of your app and unlock new possibilities. - Providing exceptional customer support and communication strengthens user relationships. - Expanding your app to global markets requires localization and understanding cultural considerations. - Utilizing SEO and ASO increases app visibility and attracts more organic downloads. - Building a community around your app fosters user engagement, loyalty, and feedback. - Creating engaging app content enhances user experience and encourages user interaction. - Understanding app store guidelines and policies ensures compliance and app store visibility. - Harnessing the power of artificial intelligence and automation opens new avenues for no code app development. - Integrating APIs and web services enhances the functionalities of no code apps. - The future of no code development holds exciting possibilities and advancements.

NEXT STEPS

Now that you have gained a comprehensive understanding of no code app development, it's time to take the next steps on your journey. Here are some recommendations to guide you: 1. Refine Your Idea: Take a moment to reflect on your app idea and assess its potential. Conduct market research, gather user feedback, and iterate on your concept accordingly. 2. Choose the Right No Code Platform: Evaluate different no code platforms based on their features, ease of use, scalability, integration capabilities, and support. Choose a platform that aligns with your app requirements, budget, and long-term goals. 3. Create Your MVP: Following the principles discussed in Chapter 3, build your Minimum Viable Product (MVP) using the chosen no code platform. Focus on the essential features and simplify the user interface to ensure a smooth user experience. 4. Gather User Feedback: Launch your MVP and gather feedback from users. Analyze the feedback, identify areas for improvement, and iterate on your app based on user insights. Engage with your user community and build a loyal user base. 5. Implement Monetization Strategies: Based on Chapter 7, explore different monetization models and implement the one that suits your app category, user preferences, and value proposition. Continuously analyze and optimize your monetization strategies to maximize revenue. 6. Market and Promote Your App: Leverage the marketing and promotion strategies discussed in Chapter 8 to increase app visibility. Utilize social media, content marketing, paid advertising, and influencer marketing to attract users and expand your user base. 7. Continuously Iterate and Improve: Embrace an iterative mindset and continuously seek feedback from your users. Pay attention to market trends and evolving user needs. Regularly update your app, add new features, and refine existing ones to stay relevant and competitive. 8. Stay Up-to-date: Stay informed about emerging technologies, new features in no code platforms, and industry trends. Keep learning and adapting to the evolving landscape of no code app development. Remember, building a successful app takes time, effort, and continuous learning. Embrace the challenges along the way and stay motivated. With determination and creativity, you have the potential to create remarkable no code apps. Thank you for joining us on this journey through the world of no code app development. We hope this book has provided you with the knowledge and inspiration you need to excel in this exciting field. Wishing you all the best in your future endeavors! Note: This book is meant to serve as a guide, and the landscape of no code development is continuously evolving. Stay curious, continue exploring, and adapt your strategies based on the latest advancements and market trends.